BODY DYNAMICS

JOHN MAC ARTHUR, JR.

While this book is designed for the reader's personal enjoyment and profit, it is also intended for group study. A Leader's Guide with Victor Multiuse Transparency Masters is available from your local bookstore or from the publisher.

VICTOR
BOOKS a division of SP Publications, Inc.
WHEATON. ILLINOIS 60187

Offices also in
Whitby, Ontario, Canada
Amersham-on-the-Hill, Bucks, England

Second printing, 1983

Most of the Scripture quotations in this book are from the *King James Version*. Other quotations are from the *New American Standard Bible* (NASB), © 1960, 1962, 1963, 1968, 1971, 1972, 1973, 1975, 1977 by The Lockman Foundation, LaHabra, California; *The New Berkeley Version in Modern English* (BERK), © 1969 by Zondervan Publishing House; *The New Testament in Modern English* (PH), © 1958, J. B. Phillips, The Macmillan Company; and *The Holy Bible: Revised Standard Version* (RSV), © 1952 by the Division of Christian Education of the National Council of Churches of Christ in the United States. Used by Permission.

Recommended Dewey Decimal Classification: 262.77
    Suggested Subject Headings: THE CHURCH—THE BODY OF CHRIST, CHRISTIAN DOCTRINE.

Library of Congress Catalog Card Number: 81-86292
ISBN: 0-88207-360-5

CONTENTS

To my beloved Patricia,
who ministers to me most.

INTRODUCTION

Sally went to London to die. The courts had decided she was an unfit mother and had given the three children to her husband. Her life had been one of drugs, swinging parties, prostitution, perversion, abortions, money, and jet-setting. She had been excommunicated from the Mormon church. At the American Express window, she met Jenny, one of the Manson family girls, the one who had smuggled dope into the Los Angeles jail for Charlie Manson. But now Jenny was different—Jesus Christ had seen to that. She knew she could help Sally. Francis Schaeffer was in London and the two girls finally found him. That was the beginning of the beginning for Sally. She met Jesus Christ.

Tom was crazed, incensed. His wife had been unfaithful, and he was after the man. For two days, with gun in hand, he chased his victim, while police pursued. His wife was in my office, asking me to pray. In panic and frustration, he came home, fell on the floor—and for three hours wrestled with his anguish until he finally cried out to God. Liberty and peace came. Tom received the Saviour.

They weren't a family. They were three sick, separated, and broken lives who happened to have the same last name and to eat at the same table—sometimes. The boys were drug addicts, Dad was a drunk. Nobody cared. Then a kid on the corner told them the Good News of salvation. The Heaths are a family now, in Christ.

Phil was different, very different. He had all the best—the right family, the right money, the right girl, the right education

(Harvard Law School). Before he was 30 he had the job offer of a lifetime—the big money, the whole American dream. But in it all, he put Jesus Christ first.

An embalmer by profession, Dave was a guy who looked as if he had missed it all. Lonely, no family, no meaning. At 21 he sat in his car, put a gun to his head, and pumped in three bullets. Blood was everywhere, but not death. In his semiconscious state, thoughts of Jesus came back and Dave yielded to Him. Two bullets and a large hole are still in his skull. It all affected his brain, his coordination, and his eternal soul.

Each of these stories is a biography by a divine author. I know these people, teach them every week, and pray for and with them. They had nothing, humanly, to bind them together until Jesus Christ made them one fellowship.

Sally went from London to L'Abri Fellowship in Switzerland. There she met Jeff, a young man with whom I had shared some of my life and teaching. He told her of our ministry and the fact that she could find a growing experience in our fellowship. Several months later she began the long trip here. At the London airport she discovered she had miscalculated and was short about $10 for her ticket to Los Angeles. Again she met Jeff, who had just found the amount she needed lying on the ground. Together they flew to Los Angeles. We met one Sunday soon after that, and she became part of our fellowship. She is involved now, ministering her gifts to children as well as helping young people solve their problems.

Tom came to church the Sunday after his dramatic chase; his wife brought him. We met and he began to come regularly to Bible study. He devoured the Word like a starving man and grew so rapidly that in a few months he was building up his own library of Bible study tools and using them. Then came the desire to teach and verification by the Body that he had the gift of teaching. A Sunday School class of 70 adults was next, then home Bible studies and prayer groups. God gave him great concern for missions, and that became his service. All this happened in less than two years.

8

The Heaths were reached by a young man from our fellowship who shared Christ with one son who witnessed to his brother. The boys' lives began to speak to their dad. He came to see me, responded to Christ, and became part of the miracle on the block—a miracle that has touched more than 20 people. Immediately they began to participate in the fellowship, were taught and ministered to by the Body. Now they are involved in bringing drug addicts to Christ.

Phil came to us because he heard we taught the Word. He became involved in ministering his gifts among the newly married and soon was leading that fastest-growing part of our fellowship. Door-to-door evangelism teams and prayer groups function weekly under his leadership. He was offered a high-paying position with one of the world's largest corporations. I'll never forget the letter he sent them; it said, in effect, that he could not accept their kind and generous offer because he felt committed to the Lord's work in his Bible class. I imagined their shock.

Dave came because someone told him he could find fellowship and love here. He gave as much as he found. He began by being available to drive his car for junior high outings; then he entered all their activities and soon started to faithfully study the Word, equipping himself for teaching them. He taught a group of boys, chauffeured them, heard their problems, and loved them; and it was mutual. We talked a lot about missions, and prayed. After a while the circumstances matched his heart's desire, and he began his training for service in another land as God directs.

All in this group meet to pray for each other and for all the saints, as well as those to whom they witness. They are hippies, housewives, low-riders, lawyers, teachers, students, surfers, musicians, doctors, businessmen, and factory workers caring for each other and reaching the world for Jesus Christ. Outside of Him, they have nothing in common; in Him, they are one in every way.

This is the Body—the Church. The blueprint for it is the theme of this book.

1
THE CHURCH: ONE BODY

(1 Corinthians 12:12-14)

What is the Church? The answers are legion. Churches, as we think of them, vary from well-structured, wealthy, highly organized institutions to underground cell groups with no money or structure.

But what is the *biblical* description of the Church? How do we express its identity and fulfill Christ's desire for it?

To begin, there are various biblical metaphors for the Church—Family, Bride, Vineyard, Temple, Building, Kingdom, and Flock, but most specifically, a Body.

The Church is the Body of Christ. Other metaphors have Old Testament equivalents, but this one does not. The concept does not even exist in the Old Testament. The Body is the Church's unique position in Christ.

The Church is not a physical building, but a group of believers; not a denomination, sect, or association, but a spiritual Body. The Church is not an organization, but a *koinonia*—a communion, a fellowship that includes all believers. This unique metaphor forms the basis of our study.

Undergirding the scriptural teaching about the Body of Christ is the concept of *unity*. "For as the Body is one and has many members, and all the members of that one Body, being many, are one Body: so also is Christ" (1 Cor. 12:12).

11

Paul refers to the physical body and says, in effect, "You know that a physical being must be one. You cannot put parts of a Body in a heap and tell the heap to do something. You cannot say to those disconnected members, 'Pull yourselves together and function.' "

A body is made up of members functioning together. I cannot say my hand is so gifted I will cut it off and send it alone to do a job. The hand would no longer be gifted; if I cut it off, it would die. Thus the essence of the body is unity.

In the Church Body, Christ is the head, and the head is the life. Looking at the metaphor from a different perspective, you can cut off a hand or an arm, but the head will maintain life. If you cut off the head, life is gone, and the same is true in the Body of Christ. "Christ is the head of the Church" (Eph. 5:23). Some people think they are the heads of their churches, but believers are one in Christ, receiving all resources—strength, wisdom, and instructions—from the same head.

How does a person enter the Body of Christ? "For by one Spirit are we all baptized into one Body, whether we be Jews or Gentiles, whether we be bond or free; and have been all made to drink into one Spirit" (1 Cor. 12:12-13).

Paul refers to "one Body" four times to emphasize Body unity (12:12-13). Christians are one. Salvation is the initial point of unity. Christians are united because they are all baptized by one Spirit into one Body.

People often ask, "What is the baptism of the Holy Spirit?" It is God's Spirit placing a believer into the Body of Christ. "By one Spirit are we *all* baptized into one Body" (12:13). A Christian comes into the Body of Christ at the moment of his salvation, being placed there by the energy of the Spirit. From the time he receives Jesus Christ he is a part of Christ's Body. Not only is he put there, but he has the same indwelling Spirit as other members of the Body.

So the Spirit regenerates all believers, places them in the Body of Christ, and indwells them. Every Christian? Yes. "If any man have not the Spirit of Christ, he is none of His" (Rom. 8:9). There is no such thing as a believer who doesn't have the Holy Spirit. Notice how Paul reminded the Ephesians "to keep the unity of the Spirit in the bond of peace" (Eph. 4:3) because the same Spirit who regenerates Christians and baptizes them into the Body, also indwells them.

One in the Spirit

The Church's unity, then, is not based on an artificial, organizational relationship. Nor on the fact that people are churchgoers. Rather, all believers have been identified in the work of a single Spirit. We are one in the Spirit.

Even though Christians are one in the Body of Christ, they have a tendency to pull apart and to isolate themselves in smaller groups who act and think the same way. It's possible for Christians to go to the same church meetings, sit together, and even talk superficially, but at heart still be far from each other. They are tightly closed to most fellow believers, even though they may be open to a few. They have not learned to express oneness in practical ways. They operate contrary to the way the Body is supposed to function, and as a result the whole Body is hindered. Much of our ministry involves getting people who are theoretically one back together experientially, as God intended.

Super saints do not exist. One minister said, "The Church is so cold and the Body so dead, that when someone arrives with a 98.6° temperature, we think he's sick. We think he has a fever, when actually he is normal." To be totally committed to Jesus Christ and totally absorbed in the Spirit's ministry is not to be super; it's to be normal.

There are no great members in the Body. No one can come in and say, "Well, how did you get here? I did this and 49 of these and 74 of those, and I got here." No, he didn't. He came by one Spirit into one Body, as everyone else did. That's the point of Christian unity. If works provided the way into the Body, we would all burst with pride. Instead, every member is brought into the Body through Christ. Christians have nothing personal to boast about.

The clergy-laity dichotomy is, in that context at least,

unbiblical. As a preacher, I am no higher than a layman, except that my pulpit is raised 36 inches off the floor. I am not above another believer, and he is not above anyone else; neither is he below anyone. No hierarchy is expressed in the Body metaphor. There are varying gifts, which we will study later, but no hierarchy. The organizational chart of Christianity is simple—Christ the head of a Body. There are levels of authority (1 Tim. 5:17), but that is not to be equated with spiritual superiority. Leaders are not some kind of upper division Christians.

Every biblical metaphor of the Church, without exception, emphasizes its unity. The Church is one Bride with one husband; one Flock with one shepherd; the Branches on one vine; one Kingdom with one king; one Family with one father; one Building with one foundation; one Body with one head, Jesus Christ. There is no room for hierarchy, no room for believers to feel like either upper-class or lower-class Christians. Jesus did not say there are blue-ribbon sheep and also-rans. *Positionally,* each believer stands on the same ground in Christ.

There is no such thing as an isolated believer—one who is by himself and not part of the Body. Whether babies, young men, or mature fathers spiritually (1 John 2:12-14), whether carnal or spiritual (1 Cor. 3:16), Christians are one (1 John 2:12-14).

The Apostle Paul had to work with a church at Corinth that was badly split (1 Cor. 1:12). Some Christians said, "I am an Apollos man." Others: "Well, not me, I'm a Paul man." "You're both wrong—Cephas is in," some said. Then the pious ones spoke, "Listen, folks, I follow Christ" (1:12). Paul replied to this: "Is Christ divided?" (1:13) "Let no man glory in men" (3:21). Christians cannot say, "I follow him, or I follow that one." The apostle adds: "For all things are yours; whether Paul, or Apollos, or Cephas, or the world, or life, or death, or things present, or things to come; all are yours; and you are Christ's; and Christ is God's" (1 Cor. 3:21-23).

Christians are to end their party bickering and return to the oneness of a redeemed people who owe their distinct existence, their life together, to the fact that they were brought into one Body by one Spirit and indwelt by the same Spirit.

Becoming Like Christ

The New Testament word for church is *ekklesia,* which means "assembly" and is from a verb meaning "to call out." Christians are called apart from the world to exist as an entity. They are to lead a life worthy of His calling (Eph. 4:1), so that they become in character and conduct what they are by virtue of their union with Christ. The Christian life is the process of working out in practice the spiritual resources of the believer's position in Christ. The Church is the company of God's people, called out to live for Him.

> At that time ye were without Christ, being aliens from the commonwealth of Israel, and strangers from the covenants of promise, having no hope, and without God in the world; But now in Christ Jesus ye who sometimes were far off are made nigh by the blood of Christ. For He is our peace, who hath made both one [that is, Jew and Gentile], and hath broken down the middle wall of partition between us; Having abolished in His flesh the enmity . . . to make in Himself of twain one new man, so making peace; And that He might reconcile both unto God in one Body by the cross. . . . For through Him we both have access by one Spirit unto the Father (2:12-16, 18).

There is to be no partiality in the Church. Christ has abolished the barriers of nationality, race, class, and sex to make all believers one. "There is neither Jew nor Greek, there is neither bond nor free, there is neither male nor female, for ye are all one in Christ Jesus" (Gal. 3:28).

Some people, however, have a hard time accepting this fact and allowing it to control their lives. They don't realize that in Christ all discrimination ends. The Church that Christ has created, of which He is head, tolerates no distinctions.

During a special evangelistic effort among blacks of one community, our team was constantly under police surveillance. At one point we were arrested and fined, accused of stirring up the blacks. Then we were threatened with a public beating if we didn't stop our meetings. The chief of police was especially profane and abusive. I told him we were there only to preach Jesus Christ and asked him if he objected to that. He said he didn't and added that he himself was a Sunday School superintendent. We were released, but constantly watched until the mission was over. (I learned later that the pastor of the police chief's church had had a nervous breakdown and finally took his own life because of pressure from his people when he began to extend concern and fellowship to blacks.)

All barriers are gone. "For there is no difference between the Jew and the Greek: for the same Lord over all is rich unto all that call upon Him. For whosoever shall call upon the name of the Lord shall be saved" (Rom. 10:12-13).

Attaining unity was especially difficult in the early Church because of the separation between Jews and Gentiles. However, Paul spoke directly to this problem: "Having abolished in His flesh the enmity, even the law of commandments contained in ordinances; for to make in Himself of twain one new man, so making peace" (Eph. 2:15).

Jesus ended legalism. He abolished "the enmity," the opposition between Jew and Gentile created by the Law. The Jew was intent on keeping the Law, and he glorified himself for doing so; at the same time, he looked down on those who didn't. The Gentile was outcast. But when Jesus died on the cross, He did away with external law-keeping as a testimony to faith. The Gentile no longer was excluded. He could move into the fullness of all God's blessings. There were no restrictions.

Scripture says the Law was good in that it revealed God's holiness and man's sinfulness. When Jesus died, He fully accepted the punishment due sinners for lawbreaking, but at the same time He met all the Law's demands. The Law, therefore, could make no more claims on Jew or Gentile. And if the Law no longer keeps men from God, it doesn't separate men from each other. If Jew and Gentile were to be brought together, the enmity had to be abolished. That's what happened when Jesus died and rose from the dead. In place of the old animosity, Christ created "one new man."

No Distinctions in the Body

In France during World War II, some GIs took the body of a buddy to a local cemetery. They were stopped by a priest, who said, "Sorry, boys, you can't bury your friend here if he's not a Catholic." Though discouraged, the GIs didn't give up; they decided to bury him outside the cemetery fence. Next morning when they went to pay their last respects at the grave, they couldn't find it. After looking for an hour, they asked the priest about it. He explained: "Well, the first part of the night I stayed awake, sorry for what I had told you. The second part of the night I spent moving the fence."

Jesus, in effect, moved the fence and included every believer in God's promises, which are received by faith apart from the works of the Law. He opened a common ground for all people to come to a knowledge of God. This means there is no reason for Christians not to love each other. Christ has removed human distinctions. In the "one new man" there is a different quality of existence; there has never been anything like the Body of Christ.

Paul in his writings calls Christians fellow heirs, fellow members, fellow partakers, and fellow citizens. All these terms emphasize the unity of the Body. Christians, therefore, are not to cut themselves off from fellow believers. Rather, their responsibility is to move into the mainstream of Body life. Some Christians, when they go to church, just sit, as if to say, "Well, God, I know You're really blessed by my being here." They don't know what it means to live in the vitality and nourishment received from Christ's Body. In effect, though sharing the same identity by virtue of their faith, they do not share the same practice. They weaken the Body. Their failure to grow in their commitment affects everyone, because other believers try to compensate for their isolation and failure to serve.

Jesus wanted all believers to experience unity. And so He prayed to His Father, "Neither pray I for these alone [the disciples], but for them also which shall believe on Me through their word; That they all may be one; as Thou, Father, art in Me, and I in Thee, that they also may be one in Us: that the world may believe that Thou has sent Me and the glory which Thou gavest Me I have given them; that they may be one, even as We are one" (John 17:20-22).

His glory is the Holy Spirit (1 Peter 4:14) and the presence of the Holy Spirit is the believer's point of unity. "I in them, and Thou in Me, that they may be made perfect in one; and that the world may know that Thou hast sent Me, and hast loved them, as Thou hast loved Me" (John 17:23).

When are Christians going to turn this world upside down? When are they going to shatter the complacency of this world? When they experience oneness! If a local congregation becomes one in body energy and begins to minister to the needs of each Christian with super-sensitive unity, the world will be astounded with the results. That local church will release the unity and the energy of the Holy Spirit.

Humility Is a Key to Oneness

How does Christian oneness work? Two keys are *humility* and *love*. Jesus prayed that Christians would be one. Paul desired it, but evidently the Christians at Philippi hadn't found it. "Fulfill ye my joy, that ye be likeminded, having the same love, being of one accord, of one mind" (Phil. 2:2). What mind is he referring to? "Let this mind be in you, which was also in Christ Jesus" (2:5). Christians are to have the mind of Christ. "Who, being in the form of God, thought it not robbery to be equal with God: But made Himself of no reputation, and took upon Him the form of a servant, and was made in the likeness of men: And being found in fashion as a man, He humbled Himself, and became obedient unto death, even the death of the cross" (2:6-8).

The mind of Christ is humility. "Look not every man on his own things, but every man also on the things of others" (2:4).

Can you imagine what would happen if all Christians cared more for others than themselves? Each Christian would get the care he needs. Each would have someone caring for him. Many Christians spend so much time on themselves that no one can tolerate caring for them. If Christians ever learn—and by God's Spirit they can—to care for each other, they will be consumed by this attitude. This is the mind of humility. No wounded egos, no stepped-on toes, no "I'm not speaking to Mrs. So-and-so anymore," no "That is the last time I'll do. . . ." Such attitudes reflect ego, not humility.

Christ never tried to maintain His ego. Mockers spat on Him, and He just stood there. They nailed Him to a cross, and He hanged there. He didn't say, "You can't do this to Me, I won't tolerate it." The mind of humility says, "If this means your salvation and your benefit and blessing, I'll suffer because I care about you." That is something of a foreign idea to some contemporary Christian experience, but it is what the body concept is all about. Selfless Paul had this in mind: "If I be offered upon the sacrifice and service of your faith, I joy" (Phil. 2:17). He was expendable for the sake of others. And he exhorts us: "For I say, through the grace given unto me, to every man that is among you, not to think of himself more highly than he ought to think. . . . For as we have many members in one Body" (Rom. 12:3-4). All Christians are in Christ's Body. They experience unity by thinking about others instead of themselves. Christians need not worry about their egos; they need not worry about their petty thoughts. They can start by reaching out and touching someone's life. Christians are one, and the point of contact for their unity is humility.

How far should humility go? A Christian could get trampled. So get trampled! God can restore you. Paul condemns a Christian who sues another Christian, goes to court, and hassles publicly with him. "Now therefore there is utterly a fault among you, because ye go to law one with another. Why do ye not rather take wrong? Why do ye not rather suffer yourselves to be defrauded? Nay, ye do wrong, and defraud, and that your brethren" (1 Cor. 6:7-8).

Paul says Christians are to care so much for each other that they are less concerned about what happens to themselves. A brother may be defrauded but another brother should pick him up, because a caring person often gets back the love he gives. Paul adds that if he dies in ministering to others, that is only "gain" (see Phil. 1:21). Each of us is expendable for the other.

Love Is Another Key
Along with humility, love is needed to experience Christian oneness. "A new commandment I give unto you, that ye love one another" (John 13:34). This love doesn't depend on circumstances or what one does. It is not selective or based on attractiveness.

Sometimes one believer will say of another, "I love her in the Lord." This is the same as saying, "I hate her." It is as if a Christian had a little valve and squirted the other person with eight drops of divine love, unmixed with his own, and then shut it off. But, in truth, either we love another or we don't. Jesus said love is not an option, but a new commandment. Christians don't have a natural capacity to love everyone, but "the love of God is shed abroad in our hearts" (Rom. 5:5).

How are Christians to love? "As I have loved you . . . ye also love one another. By this shall all men know that ye are My disciples, if ye have love one to another" (John 13:34-35). Christ had just shown love to them by washing their feet. Such love is not an emotion, but an act of selfless, sacrificial service to meet someone's need.

Christians may convince the world that Jesus is real by loving one another in this way. The greatest evangelism in the world is not having a big revival; it is having so much love that the world can't figure it out. The mark of Christian unity is love toward all believers. Paul prayed, "The Lord make you to increase and abound in love one toward another"

(1 Thes. 3:12). Another apostle wrote, "This is the message that ye heard from the beginning, that we should love one another" (1 John 3:11).

Do Christians really love as Christ loved? Or are we so protective of our egos that every time something goes wrong we retaliate and get bitter? How do we react when everything isn't the way we think it should be, if sister So-and-so and brother So-and-so irritate us? Are we angry and bitter or are we kind and loving?

The love which should characterize Christian unity causes one believer to go to his brother and say, "Brother, I have had a bitterness against you, and I want to ask you to forgive me. I want to begin to love you." Concern for Church unity also says, "Brother, I forgive you." It says, "I'm sorry, brother." It doesn't criticize others to build up oneself. It loves no matter the cost—whether money, prestige, or position. It may require repentance and confession, and making it right with a fellow believer.

The Church is not only unified, it is also diversified—Christians are one and yet they are many. "For the Body is not one member, but many" (1 Cor. 12:14).

The human body is one, and yet there are arms, fingers, and all the various parts and organs, each with unique functions, operating distinctly and yet as one. Similarly, there is *diversity* within the Body of Christ. Christians are all different.

Exercising Gifts

Christians have received different gifts, and the measure of faith to go with each gift. In other words, if God gives a Christian a spiritual gift, He gives him sufficient faith to exercise it. The Body needs different gifts. Christians need to complement each other; no one can be everything. I am gifted to do one thing, someone else to do another, and we minister to each other for the Body's health. Any organ that doesn't function cripples the whole Body.

The Body of Christ, then, is marked by diversity and unity.

"There are diversities of operation, but it is the same God which worketh all in all. . . . But all these worketh that one and the selfsame Spirit, dividing to every man severally as He will" (1 Cor. 12:6, 11).

So that all believers may minister to each other, the Spirit has apportioned gifts in beautiful balance. If a Christian does not use his gift, the Body is cheated, but as all believers are being ministered to and are ministering their gifts, they all are maturing and enjoying a full complement of gifts.

Football players know that team unity is the basic ingredient in winning. Each player must carry out his assignment for the success of the whole. Imagine a sportscaster interviewing a player. The player says the team is one, really one, so much so that everyone has decided to play quarterback. That is not unity, it is chaos. The team doesn't need 11 quarterbacks. There must be diversity in the midst of basic harmony. The team needs ends, tackles, guards, a center, and backs. Each must be fully committed to his unique place on the team if there's to be unity. My coach used to say, "If you believe that your position is the most important one on the field, and if you play it that way on every play, we can't be beaten!"

Diversity is vital to the functioning of the Church. Spiritual gifts are a sovereign, God-given blessing. A Christian must use his. He may say, "Well, I applied to the Sunday School and they don't need a third-grade teacher." That shouldn't stop him. The Bible doesn't say, "Find an organization and assign your gift to it." Every believer can find a place to use his gift. There are many opportunities in the church program and outside it. If a Christian has the gift of helps, for example, he may find someone in his neighborhood who needs help. If he has the gift of teaching, he may exercise it with only one or two children in his neighborhood. Many Christians are idle, though they have spiritual gifts that the Body of Christ is craving. Needs are so great that every Christian can minister his gifts.

How can a Christian know his gift? By reading and studying those described in the Scriptures (Rom. 12 and 1 Cor. 12).

Then pray and ask for the Holy Spirit's leading. His leading will confirm what the Christian likes to do and what he does with a measure of success and joy. If he loves to work with people, perhaps he has the gift of helps. If he is a good organizer, perhaps he has the gift of administration or ruling. The Christian is not to become preoccupied, however, with the academics of gifts. If he is filled with the Holy Spirit, the Spirit's gifts will operate freely, and the Christian will be able to identify his gift. Other members of the Body will be able to verify his gifts.

A Christian doesn't necessarily need the structured organization to minister his gifts. I've told my congregation, "You who are working here in the local congregation, this is where God has put you—use your gifts. But if you find no opening, if there is no place for you, go and minister to someone."

The Body of Christ must also have *harmony* in the ministering of gifts.

If the foot shall say, "Because I am not the hand, I am not of the Body"; is it therefore not of the Body? And if the ear shall say, "Because I am not the eye, I am not of the Body"; is it therefore not of the Body? If the whole Body were an eye, where were the hearing? If the whole were hearing, where were the smelling? But now hath God set the members every one of them in the Body, as it hath pleased Him. And if they were all one member, where were the Body? But now are they many members, yet but one Body. And the eye cannot say unto the hand, "I have no need of thee": nor again the head to the feet, "I have no need of you." Nay, much more those members of the Body, which seem to be more feeble, are necessary: And those members of the Body, which we think to be less honorable, upon these we bestow more abundant honor; and our uncomely parts have more abundant comeliness. For our comely parts have no need: but God hath tempered the Body together, having given more abundant honor to that part which lacked: That there should be no schism in the Body; but that the members should have the same care one for another (1 Cor. 12:15-25).

This passage shows the Christian's attitude of respect for each fellow member. Each Christian is to be content with his gifts and harmonize with the whole Body. It is not always the most obvious gift that is most critical. A beautiful mouth is nice, an ugly lung is necessary, and so is a thumb.

In the Body of Christ there is unity, diversity, and harmony. To be a healthy Body, the Church needs every Christian—not necessarily more structure or more organization. Rather, the Church needs more Body unity and more Body ministry. Jesus prayed for this.

Christian unity is the unity of the Spirit, not of the denomination or the organization. There will be true Church unity when Christians humble themselves, when they work for the interests of others, when they love with selfless love and when they minister their gifts in harmony.

2
GOD'S ETERNAL MASTER PLAN

(Ephesians 1:3-14)

Though we are focusing on the aspects of the Body of Christ, which are part of the believer's life on earth, the Body really transcends place and time. It was formed in the timelessness of eternity by the sovereign design of Almighty God. God has "made known unto us the mystery [sacred secret, hidden in the Old Testament] of His will . . . That in the dispensation of the fullness of times He might gather together in one all things in Christ" (Eph. 1:9-10). "How that by revelation He made known unto me the mystery . . . Which in other ages was not made known unto the sons of men, as it is now revealed unto His holy apostles and prophets by the Spirit" (3:3, 5).

Then Paul explains "that the Gentiles should be fellow heirs, and members of the same Body" (3:6). His mission, he goes on to say, is "to make all men see what is the fellowship of the mystery" (3:9). This is the mystery of the Body—that Jew and Gentile have been gathered together and molded into a single Body, of which Christ is the head. God is forming a Body of Jew and Gentile, rich and poor, learned and unlearned, male and female, slave and free—"one new man" (2:15).

A mystery in the biblical sense is a truth which God ordained in eternity past and hid, to be revealed at a certain time. Before any of us was born, before the earth was formed,

God planned the Body of Christ (1:3-6). Paul ascribes the forming of the mystery Body to eternity past.

To realize that God loved me and placed me within the Body of Christ in His own master plan, before the world was even created, is cause for rejoicing. Thinking of this truth caused Paul to burst out in a great song of praise (1:3-14) which is one sentence of 200 words in the Greek, and may be the longest sentence in religious literature. It is connected, yet disconnected, and since it is a complicated sentence, it must be taken piece by piece.

This lyrical song of praise flows from Paul's heart. His mind goes from glory to glory, from gift to gift, from wonder to wonder. He talks about election, sanctification, foreordination, identification, adoption, acceptance, redemption, sanctification, enrichment, enlightenment, glorification, inheritance, the sealing of the Holy Spirit. All the cardinal doctrines are included in his song of praise, as he reviews how God formed the Body before the world began.

He constantly gives God the glory: "to the praise of the glory of His grace" (1:6); "that we should be to the praise of His glory" (1:12); "unto the praise of His glory" (1:14). The song of praise actually has three parts: first, the past aspect of God's eternal formation of the Body (1:4-6); then the present aspect (1:6-11); and finally the future aspect (1:12-14). God's eternal plan for the Body has three parts: the past—election; the present—redemption; the future—inheritance.

Paul presents seven facts about God's formation of the Body in eternity past (1:4-6). Seven is often God's number for perfection and completion. Paul reveals (1) the method by which the Body was elected; (2) the objects of God's election; (3) the time of election; (4) the purpose of the Body; (5) the motive for God's election; (6) the result of His election, and (7) the goal of the Body.

The Method

"According as He hath chosen us in Him" (1:4). That describes the method. He didn't draw straws; He chose by His sovereign will who would be in the Body of Christ. Election was His plan. The Greek root for "chosen" is *eklego,* meaning "to call out" or "to elect." He chose totally apart from human will and purely on the basis of His sovereignty. Since the Greek verb for "chosen" is in the middle voice and thus reflexive the meaning is "according as He hath chosen us for Himself." God acted totally independent of any outside influence. Paul's heart overflowed at such a glorious thought. He blessed God for choosing unworthy sinners.

God wrote names in the Book of Life before the world began. "The beast that thou sawest was, and is not, and shall ascend out of the bottomless pit, and go into perdition; and they that dwell on the earth shall wonder, whose names were not written in the Book of Life from the foundation of the world" (Rev. 17:8). (See Rev. 20:15.)

Election is the first cause of all blessing; that is why Paul begins with it. The doctrine of election runs through the whole Bible. God does everything according to His own will and mind. Israel was elect (Ex. 6). The angels were elect (1 Tim. 5:21). Christ was elect (1 Peter 2:6). Certain believers were elected for certain tasks (Acts 9:15). The forming of the Body is by God's choice.

Jesus said to His disciples, "Ye have not chosen Me, but I have chosen you, and ordained you" (John 15:16). And in the same Gospel, "But as many as received Him, to them gave He power to become the sons of God, even to them that believe on His name; Which were born, not of blood, nor of the will of the flesh, nor of the will of man, but of God" (John 1:12-13).

Also, in the epistles we read, "Who hath saved us, and called us with an holy calling, not according to our works, but according to His own purpose and grace, which was given us in Christ Jesus before the world began" (2 Tim. 1:9), and, "Therefore I endure all things for the elect's sakes, that they may also obtain the salvation which is in Christ Jesus with eternal glory" (2 Tim. 2:10), and finally, "We are bound to give thanks alway to God for you, brethren beloved of the Lord, because God hath from the beginning chosen you to salvation" (2 Thes. 2:13).

Despite some Christians' fears, these statements of God's

election of believers are not in the Bible to cause a controversy. Election is a fact. It does not exclude the responsibility of man. It does not exclude personal response by faith. Jesus said, "Him that cometh to Me I will in no wise cast out" (John 6:37). "But those two concepts don't go together," you say. You're right. However, they both are true separately—election and human responsibility—and they form a paradox. But there is no paradox in the mind of God. He understands it perfectly; we don't. Our faith and salvation rest entirely on the election of God, and yet the day a person comes to Jesus Christ, he comes because he desires to.

If salvation depends on man, then praise to God is ridiculous. If it depends on us, we would sing, "Praise me, glory to me in the highest." But, in truth, our praise to God is all the more appropriate because in forming the Body before the world began, He chose us by a sovereign decree apart from works of man. How we must praise Him for that! The doctrine of election allows God to be God.

How can God choose some, offer salvation to everyone, and then hold people responsible who weren't chosen? I don't know. But it is a mystery only to us. I don't know how God resolves it, but I am content to leave it with Him. The Bible teaches election and human responsibility. I have heard people say that the truth is somewhere in the middle. Not so! The truth is at both extremes—not a mishmash in the middle. Let God be God and man be man. I say, praise God for His secrets. I get excited knowing that God loved me before I was born.

The Objects

"According as He hath chosen us" (Eph. 1:4). Who are the "us"? Please remember this, God didn't choose everyone to salvation. The Bible never teaches that. The "us" in this verse are Christian believers. Jesus said, "And this is the Father's will which hath sent Me, that of all that He hath given Me I should lose nothing" (John 6:39). There is a Body which God has chosen to be a gift to Jesus Christ. Every believer is part of that love gift to Christ. He is the gift of a Father's love to His

Son. "For the children being not yet born, neither having done any good or evil, that the purpose of God according to election might stand" (Rom. 9:11).

God actually determines salvation before the children are born. To those who claim that this is unjust, Paul answers, "What shall we say then? Is there unrighteousness with God? [Is this unfair?] God forbid. For He saith to Moses, 'I will have mercy on whom I will have mercy, and I will have compassion on whom I will have compassion'" (9:14-15), and "Therefore hath He mercy on whom He will have mercy, and whom He will hardeneth. Thou wilt say then unto me, 'Why doth He yet find fault? For who hath resisted His will?'" (9:18-19)

Why would God find fault in us if He didn't choose us? Paul's answer is, "O man, who are thou that repliest against God? [You have no right to question God.] Shall the thing formed say to Him that formed it, 'Why hast thou made me thus?'" (9:20)

Does the clay jump up and ask the potter why it looks the way it does? Not at all. Some may say, "That is terribly cold and calculating." It is only one side of God's sovereign election. "That if thou shalt confess with thy mouth the Lord Jesus and shalt believe in thine heart that God hath raised Him from the dead, thou shalt be saved" (10:9).

Do you read election in that verse? No, it is not there. "For with the heart man believeth unto righteousness; and with the mouth confession is made unto salvation. For the Scripture saith, 'Whosoever believeth on Him shall not be ashamed.' . . . For 'whosoever shall call upon the name of the Lord shall be saved'" (10:10-11, 13).

How these two sides of the truth come together is not our problem to resolve—it is for God to resolve. I don't understand it, but I rejoice in it.

The Time

Paul says it was "before the foundation of the world" (Eph. 1:4). In eternity past God laid out all the plans. "Known unto God are all His works from the beginning of the world" (Acts 15:18). How much did God plan? Everything. He formed the Body in eternity past. "Then shall the King say unto them on His right hand, 'Come, ye blessed of My Father, inherit the kingdom prepared for you from the foundation of the world'" (Matt. 25:34). He laid the whole plan at once; the coming of Jesus Christ was part of it. "But with the precious blood of Christ, as of a lamb without blemish and without spot: Who verily was foreordained before the foundation of the world" (1 Peter 1:19-20). Christ is called "the Lamb slain from the foundation of the world" (Rev. 13:8).

The Purpose
Why did God do it? "According as He hath chosen us in Him before the foundation of the world, that we should be holy and without blemish before Him" (Eph. 1:4).

God wants us to be "before Him," in His own presence. God wants our fellowship. The whole Body of Christ is designed for fellowship with the Father (John 14:3; 17:24; 1 John 1:3).

Man must meet some prerequisites if he is to have fellowship with God. Holiness is one. God chose believers to make them holy, that they may enter His presence. Anything unholy is removed from God's presence. "Christ also loved the Church, and gave Himself for it; that He might sanctify and cleanse it with the washing of water by the Word, that He might present it to Himself a glorious Church, not having spot, or wrinkle, or any such thing; but that it should be holy and without blemish" (Eph. 5:27).

Paul also says Christians were chosen to be "without blame" (1:4). The Greek word amomos, is used of a perfect lamb brought to the temple sacrifice. Man must be spotless to have fellowship with God. Since only Jesus Christ is spotless, God had to give to Christians the spotlessness of Christ. Only in Christ can we go before God and enjoy fellowship with Him. Those who love Him are now in that fellowship.

Election doesn't carry us halfway, but all the way to God. Some have taught that God elects you—that gets you halfway —and then you believe and that takes you the rest of the way. Others say that God casts a vote for you, the devil casts a vote against you, and you cast the deciding vote. No! That would make man, God, and the devil equal. Election takes you to holiness; it makes you without blemish, cleansed from every sin and brought into the presence of God.

The Motive
Why did God do all this? Love motivated the formation of the Body. Love generated election. "In love: Having predestinated us" (1:5).

Some people see predestination as harsh doctrine. It came from the warmth of God's love. The whole world deserved hell; only love chose us. Look at your sin and worthlessness; then remember that even before you existed, God loved you and chose you. "Herein is love, not that we loved God, but that He loved us" (1 John 4:10). He loved us and set His love on us. It is exciting beyond words to know that God loves me and has loved me since eternity past. That is security. "Come, ye blessed of My Father, inherit the kingdom prepared for you from the foundation of the world" (Matt. 25:34). "All that the Father giveth Me shall come to Me . . . of all that He hath given Me I should lose nothing" (John 6:37, 39).

The Result
When we love someone, we naturally want him as close to us as possible. God loved us so much that He made us His children, adopting us into His Family. Adoption is the result of election.

"In love He predestined us in Jesus Christ for His sonship" (Eph. 1:5, BERK). That is as close as God could get us to Himself. Second-class sons? No. Christ is not ashamed to call us His "brethren" (Heb. 2:11) and "joint-heirs" (Rom. 8:17).

In Roman days, when a child was adopted, he received every right of a born son. If the adopted one was in debt or in trouble for crime, the moment he was adopted into a Roman family everything in his past was wiped clean. He had no debts; owed nothing to society, his crime was forgotten, and he started a new life. Everything his new father possessed was rightfully his.

Why did God want to redeem us?

"But when the fullness of the time was come, God sent forth His Son, made of a woman, made under the Law, to redeem them that were under the Law, that we might receive the adoption of sons. And because ye are sons, God hath sent forth the Spirit of His Son into your hearts, crying, 'Abba, Father.' Wherefore thou art no more a servant, but a son; and if a son, then an heir of God through Christ" (Gal. 4:4-7).

This gives the believer insight into his identity. When God says the believer is a son, it means something. All the Father's love, all His spiritual blessings belong to the Christian. The Father's care and the Father's gifts are his; boldness to enter the Father's presence and to say "Father" in an intimate way; the promise of an inheritance; a place in the Father's house; the rights and privileges of sonship. All this is true of every Christian because God in eternity past chose us to be adopted into His Family.

The Goal
In the ultimate sense, what does it mean to God to have us as sons? "According to the good pleasure of His will, to the praise of the glory of His grace" (Eph. 1:5-6) and "the praise of His glory" (1:12). That is the reason for everything. The theme runs throughout the Bible: God's glory. "For it is God which worketh in you both to will and to do of His good pleasure" (Phil. 2:13). Christians are a joy to the heart of God.

Believers need to understand that they are not insignificant people. They are specially loved by God, chosen before the world began to receive His love and blessings and to radiate Christ to the world.

Paul warns that a Christian "should not think of himself more highly than he ought to think" (Rom. 12:3), but some Christians may think too lowly. Something is wrong with a Christian if he doesn't every day bless the name of God for his place in the Body. How pathetic it is for a Christian with these glorious possessions and privileges to dabble in sin and disobedience! A Christian has no cause for a defeatist, inferior attitude. He is beloved by God, and is a part of the Body formed before the world began.

3
KNOW YOUR POSITION

(Ephesians 1:15-23)

When I was in college football, the coaches constantly drilled us with the admonition, "Play your position!" They had to say it often because when we saw action going on somewhere else on the field, we were tempted to dash over and try to grab the guy with the ball. About that time play would reverse to the spot we had just left.

One of the best players was so aggressive that he never stayed in his place. He was everywhere on the field tackling people, and invariably the wrong ones. Finally he was benched. Though he was a good athlete, he proved worthless to the team because he wouldn't stick to his position.

There's a parallel to this in Christian experience. God has put us on His team and given us both the resources and the obligation to "play" our positions in the Body of Christ. He gives us spiritual gifts for carrying out our assignments. In the football team's locker room the coaches diagram plays on a chalkboard. Everyone's position is plain to see. The plays always develop perfectly on the chalkboard, because the figures representing the players always make the right moves. On the field it's a different story.

The Christian must first find his position in the Body of Christ. He must study the chalkboard, so to speak, and see where he stands, who's on either side of him, who's behind him, who's in front of him. He cannot be an effective participant in Christian experience until he learns his place. Many Christians don't know how to live, partly because they don't know their positions.

In the first three chapters of Ephesians, the Apostle Paul presents the believer's position, the spiritual standing that God has given him in Christ. In the last three chapters Paul tells how "to play the game." Once a Christian really knows his position, his resources, and his power, he can get into the game wholeheartedly, with confidence that he can do the job. Otherwise, he will not function properly.

Basically, God's gift of salvation in Christ brings a believer into a position of righteousness. Man naturally is a sinner, separated from a holy God. But by virtue of his faith in Christ, a person can know God. Christ's perfect righteousness becomes the believer's righteousness. Though declared positionally righteous, the believer still has sins in his life. He is not righteous 100 percent of the time in his experience, but he is exhorted, on the basis of his positional righteousness, to strive for righteousness in practice.

This theme runs right through the New Testament: Christians are to become in practice what they are in position. In the Scriptures every believer is described as spiritually alive unto God, dead to sin, forgiven, righteous, a child of God, God's possession, an heir of God, blessed with all spiritual blessings, a citizen of heaven, a servant of God, free from the Law, crucified to the world, a light in the world, victorious over Satan, cleansed, holy and blameless, set free in Christ from the power of sin, secure in Christ, knowing peace and rest, led by the Holy Spirit.

"I don't always live up to those descriptions," you say. That is why in the New Testament, for every one of these statements of our position, there is a corresponding practice which Christians are to follow. For example, since the Christian is spiritually alive to God, he is told to live that new life; since he's dead to sin, he's not to give sin any place in his life; since he's forgiven, he's to count on it and not go through life feeling guilty; since he's righteous, he's to live righteously; since he's a child of God, he's told to act like God's child; since he's God's possession, he's supposed to yield to Him; since he's an heir of God, he's to add to his inheritance.

Position Is Settled

If believers would honestly study their positions, their lives would be changed. They would understand that failure in some aspect of Christian living doesn't mean they lose their position. In truth, a Christian's position is forever settled. It is unchanging, permanent. Sometimes a believer thinks that when he has done something wrong, he has blown the whole thing, that he is no longer righteous before God. That is false. Lack of growth and maturity never touch a Christian's position.

On the other hand, just as stumbling will not change a Christian's standing for the worse, neither will growth add to it for the better. Some people hold that the more mature you become in Christian experience, the more God likes you. As you grow, God becomes more gracious and loving. But God's favor does not depend on our works. "God hath saved us, and called us with an holy calling, not according to our works, but according to His own purpose and grace, which was given us in Christ Jesus before the world began" (2 Tim. 1:9).

God's total grace was extended before the world was created. We can't add one wit to His favor. From the moment of our salvation we received the absolute favor of God—there is no degree to it.

The Christian is "accepted in the beloved [Christ]" (Eph.1:6). He cannot increase or decrease in the favor of God. Nothing a Christian does, or fails to do, can change to the slightest degree his perfect standing before God.

When a normal baby is born, he has all his parts. He doesn't begin life with one leg, for example, then grow another leg in two years and a nose eight months later. The growth process doesn't add new parts, but merely strengthens existing ones. That's how it is with Christians.

When a person is created anew in Jesus Christ, he is created with all the necessary parts—nothing is missing.

Christian growth strengthens what God has positionally made us. "I know that, whatsoever God doeth, it shall be forever: nothing can be put to it, nor anything taken from it" (Ecc. 3:14).

When God does a work, it's done and we are not able to add or take away. Instead of asking God for more parts, instead of seeking to be more favorable to God, we should do what the Apostle Paul prayed that the Colossians would do: "Give thanks unto the Father, which hath made us meet [fit] to be partakers of the inheritance of the saints in light" (Col. 1:12).

The Christian is already fit. No attainment, no growth makes him any more favored or more complete. "Ye are complete in Him" (Col. 2:10). Paul is not speaking of the Christian's practice; he does not say the Christian is perfect in behavior. But because of salvation, the believer is complete in Christ.

"For by one offering He [Christ] hath perfected forever them that are sanctified" (Heb. 10:14).

Yet a person who understands his position will see changes in his life. Throughout the New Testament, there is emphasis on the believer's identity and his understanding of his positional resources. A Christian with a true self-image will be an effective Christian. The mature Christian understands who he is, relies on his positional resources, checks them out, knows what is at his disposal, then charges into the practical aspects of Christian living. Paul appeals to us to so live. "I, therefore, the prisoner of the Lord, beseech you that ye walk worthy of the vocation wherewith ye are called" (Eph. 4:1).

An interesting pattern recurs in Ephesians. In 1:1-14 Paul speaks of the believer's position, and in 1:15-23 he prays that we will understand our position. Again, in 2:1—3:12 he gives positional truth; then in 3:13-21 he prays that Christians will understand it. Twice Paul does it: Position-prayer, position-prayer. Not until chapter 4 does he get into the practice of the Christian life. The principle in Christian living, as in football is: you can't play your position until you know what it is. The Christian life is becoming in practice what we are in position.

Paul's prayer includes both thanksgiving and petition: "Wherefore I also, after I heard of your faith in the Lord Jesus, and love unto all the saints, cease not to give thanks for you, making mention of you in my prayers" (Eph. 1:15-16).

Paul was in prison in Rome but received reports from Ephesus. It had been four years since he had been there, but Christian travelers using the network of Roman roads and sea transportation brought him word. Paul and these people felt a sincere bond of love. The Ephesian believers were concerned about his arrest, and they wanted to see him. Paul's heart was full of rejoicing, especially for two things he had learned about the Ephesians: their faith in Christ and their love for one another.

After assuring the Ephesians of his thankfulness for them, Paul's prayer becomes a petition that they might understand their position in Christ (1:17). The ignorance of many Christians is tragic. The Prophet Hosea noted this: "My people are destroyed for lack of knowledge" (Hosea 4:6). They were cut off from blessing because they didn't know the facts. Many Christians stumble throughout their lives because they have no idea what their resources are.

What is more, God gives the believer equipment to understand his position and resources. The natural mind does not understand spiritual truth. If the brain were the key to spiritual understanding, the most intellectual persons would be the most Christlike. But note what Paul prays for: "That the God of our Lord Jesus Christ, the Father of glory, may give you the spirit of wisdom and revelation in the knowledge of Him" (Eph. 1:17).

The key to the verse is the word "spirit." It is not the Holy Spirit, because they have already received Him at the time of their conversions. "If any man have not the Spirit of Christ, he is none of His" (Rom. 8:9).

Is Paul speaking of the so-called human spirit? Hardly. How could a man be given a human spirit when he already has one?

The Greek word for "spirit" (*pneuma*) means "wind, breath,

and air," but it also means "an attitude, disposition, or influence." Paul was saying, in effect, "I'm praying that God will give you the attitude of wisdom and revelation" (Eph. 1:17). We use "spirit" that way in our day; someone comes into the room looking gloomy and you say, "You're in low spirits today." You mean his prevailing attitude is sad. Or, you may say, "Look at that guy! Boy, is he spirited!" You mean that his attitude is energetic, enthusiastic.

The highest thing a Christian may do in this life is give himself unstintingly and wholeheartedly to concern for "wisdom and revelation." The Holy Spirit produces the right attitude in the believer and enables him to understand God's revelation.

> But God hath revealed them unto us by His Spirit; for the Spirit searcheth all things, yea, the deep things of God. For what man knoweth the things of a man, save the spirit of man which is in him? Even so the things of God knoweth no man, but the Spirit of God. Now we have received, not the spirit of the world, but the Spirit which is of God; that we might know the things that are freely given to us of God (1 Cor. 2:10-12).

It takes the Holy Spirit to work on us, to create in us an attitude that hungers to know our resources. Every Christian needs the disposition that hungers and thirsts after the knowledge of God.

The Christian knows God through his faith in Christ but Paul's concern is for a depth of knowledge which takes more than human intellect. The Holy Spirit alone can unearth the deep things of God and open the Christian's mind to "wisdom and revelation." Revelation refers to the facts, wisdom to the practical use of facts. The apostle considers both the content and the proper use of knowledge. There's a vast difference between "a knowledge of spiritual things" and "spiritual knowledge." Many people know a lot of theology, but lack wisdom to apply the facts. Some degree of divine illumination comes with salvation, but every Christian needs to plumb the deep things of God. Paul especially wants believers to know the greatness of God's plan, the greatness of His power, and the greatness of His Son.

The Greatness of God's Plan

When a Christian has "the spirit of wisdom and revelation" in his heart, his capacity for understanding the truth is enlarged, and he will have a greater grasp of God's plan than he had before. Paul describes this process as having "the eyes of the understanding being enlightened; that ye may know what is the hope of His calling, and what the riches of the glory of His inheritance in the saints" (Eph. 1:18).

The word translated "understanding" is the Greek word *kardias,* meaning "heart." It refers to the thinking process of the inner man. The inner man must be enlightened to understand the hope of God's calling and the riches of His inheritance.

This enlightenment has nothing to do with IQ, but rather with sensitivity to the Holy Spirit. There are people on the lower rungs of the ladder academically who have keen spiritual insight. On the other hand, some on the top of the academic ladder lack spiritual insight. We see the principle of spiritual enlightenment in several Scriptures: " 'These are the words which I spake unto you, while I was yet with you, that all things must be fulfilled, which were written in the Law of Moses, and in the Prophets, and in the Psalms, concerning Me.' Then opened He their understanding, that they might understand the Scriptures" (Luke 24:44-45).

These verses describe the process between Jesus and His disciples. Divine intervention alone can unlock our spiritual understanding. The natural man cannot do it; the truths about God's plan must be supernaturally revealed.

Lydia provides another example: "And a certain woman, named Lydia, a seller of purple, of the city of Thyatira, which worshiped God, heard us: whose heart the Lord opened, that she attended unto the things which were spoken of Paul" (Acts 16:14).

The Lord opened her heart. She could not understand the spiritual truths Paul was preaching apart from the Holy Spirit's work in her heart. He is the illuminator.

Paul explains the principle: "The god of this world [the devil] hath blinded the minds of them which believe not, lest the light of the glorious Gospel of Christ, who is the image of God, should shine unto them. . . . For God, who commanded the light to shine out of darkness, hath shined in our hearts, to give the light of the knowledge of the glory of God in the face of Jesus Christ" (2 Cor. 4:4, 6). Knowing the truth is the result of God making light shine within us.

Paul then stresses that believers should understand two aspects of God's plan: the hope of His calling, and the riches of His inheritance. The little phrase, "the hope of His calling," ranges from eternity past to eternity future, covering everything in between. "Calling" refers to God's election of the believer before the foundation of the world (Eph. 1:4). Our "hope" is eternal life with Christ. Paul, in effect, prays that Christians will understand God's election in eternity past, His glory in eternity future, and all He has given the believer in between. In a word, the hope of our calling wraps up everything God has given the believer in his salvation. In another epistle the security of God's plan is revealed. "Faithful is He that calleth you, who also will do it" (1 Thes. 5:24). Our hope, our assurance is that He will do what He says.

This is the answer to a spiritual inferiority complex. In the plan of God the believer was chosen, redeemed, made holy, and glorified. He said He would do it, and He did it. His word assures our position in Christ and our resources. The secret of a proper Christian self-image is not to have an exalted view of ourselves, but the right perspective as we stand in Christ. To explore the depths of our position in Christ, we need hunger for spiritual insight, which the Holy Spirit produces in our spirit as we search the Word of God.

The second aspect of God's great plan for enlightening believers is "the riches of the glory of His inheritance in the saints." Saints, in the biblical sense, are those who have called on Christ in faith (1 Cor. 1:2). In God's master plan He has given believers an inheritance; all that God has is ours—endless riches for eternity. We are "joint-heirs with Christ" (Rom. 8:17).

It's impossible to describe precisely "the riches of the glory of His inheritance." Whatever it is, we know it is more than anyone will ever need. There is no bottom, no end to it. Indeed, Paul calls God's riches "unsearchable" (Eph. 3:8). But that doesn't keep him from talking about them—he mentions "the riches of His grace" (1:7); God being "rich in mercy" (2:4); and "the riches of His glory" (3:16).

God's riches are adequate for any situation a Christian may face. But how can the believer tap his resources? "Let the word of Christ dwell in you richly" (Col. 3:16).

If one's mind is saturated with the Word of God, unending resources will flow. It is the answer to fear, doubts, and anxiety. It is understanding our resources because we were picked to be a part of God's plan. His plan is right now for every believer, because each one is not just "in" God's plan, he *is* God's plan. Thus it is essential to have spiritual understanding of your position.

All my life I heard what I ought to do for God. I was told to be more dedicated, more committed, more consecrated; I was always being enjoined to do this, do this, do this. I got so frustrated I wondered if God had done anything for me; I wanted someone to say, "Here's what God wants to do for you." This is the great blessing of knowing our position in Christ, knowing all that's ours because we *are* God's plan. So Paul prays for the believers to understand the greatness of the plan.

The Greatness of God's Power

"And what is the exceeding greatness of His power toward us who believe, according to the working of His mighty power, which He wrought in Christ, when He raised Him from the dead, and set Him at His own right hand in the heavenly places" (Eph. 1:19-20).

It's not enough to speak of the greatness of God's power; it is "exceeding greatness." Paul uses every word he can think of that means power. Best of all, that power is "toward us"—not out there in the cosmic universe. But what is that power?

"Power" in Greek is *dunamis,* from which we get our word "dynamite." God's power in the believer is like a stick of dynamite. Christians ought to be exploding all over this world. Instead, many don't even fizzle; they may not even bother to light their fuses. They don't know that in Christ they are literally *dunamis.*

This power is "working," which is the Greek word *energeia,* from which we get our word "energy." Christians are energized by almighty power, the power that created the universe. Paul describes it as the power God used when He raised Christ from the dead and put Him at His right hand. Many Christians wonder if they have ever experienced such power. Yet that same power is unleashed in the Christian at the time of conversion. "But ye shall receive power after that the Holy Spirit is come upon you" (Acts 1:8).

God's power raised Christ and exalted Him in heaven. "Buried with Him in baptism, in which also ye are risen with Him through the faith of the operation of God, who hath raised Him from the dead" (Col. 2:12). That same kind of power is resident in the believer, according to this verse, which tells what happened to the believer when he received Jesus Christ. God showed His resurrection power at the point of the Christian's salvation; God made him alive in Christ. God's power was unleashed. What a tragedy if that power lies dormant in the believer subsequent to his conversion. "Whom we preach, warning every man, and teaching every man in all wisdom; that we may present every man perfect in Christ Jesus: Whereunto I also labor, striving according to His working, which worketh in me mightily" (Col. 1:28-29).

Paul shows how this power worked in his life as he labored to preach and teach Christ. Paul knew God's power practically in his own experience; thus he could speak of the Gospel coming "in power" (1 Thes. 1:5).

God's power is available for use now. Too many Christians, asked to do something for Jesus Christ, fumble around and wonder if they can handle it. It is sad for a Christian to suffer from an emasculated image of himself. Get a grip on who you are. You are supercharged with divine dynamite; why chug along in your Christian life at five miles an hour, when you have a unique power at your disposal. "Now unto Him that is able to do exceeding abundantly above all that we ask or think, according to the power that worketh in us" (Eph. 3:20).

It would have been great enough if Paul had said, "Christ is able to do what we ask," or, "He is able to do *above* all we can ask or think," or, "is able to do *abundantly above* all we can ask or think." But Paul goes on to define God's power at work in us as being "*exceeding* abundantly above all that we ask or think." It was this power Paul desired—"That I may know Him, and the power of His resurrection" (Phil. 3:10)—and the power he experienced—"I can do all things through Christ which strengtheneth me" (Phil. 4:13). The same may be true for every Christian!

The Greatness of God's Son

"Far above all principality, and power, and might, and dominion, and every name that is named, not only in this world, but also in that which is to come" (Eph. 1:21).

This means Christ is far above all ranks of angels, above Satan, above every power and authority in all history, or any yet to come. None is superior to Him. "And hath put all things under His feet, and gave Him to be the head over all things to the Church, which is His Body, the fullness of Him that filleth all in all" (Eph. 1:22-23).

This is a symbolic reference to the king elevated above his subjects, who bow before him. It is the picture of the believer's position in Christ. The Christian does not operate independently in this world; he is part of Christ's Body, the Church of which Christ is the head. All life flows from Him; each member functions in Him. The head needs the Body to carry out its work; the Body needs the head for direction.

When young Timothy was having such problems with intimidation, persecution, and temptation that he had stomach trouble, Paul told him directly, "Remember Jesus Christ" (2 Tim. 2:8). Yes, he was to take a little wine for his stomach trouble and he was to stir up his spiritual gifts, but Paul's supreme counsel was, "Remember your resources in Christ."

Paul did not tell Timothy to rededicate or reconsecrate himself. Timothy needed to take a fresh look at Jesus. "Remember Jesus Christ, born of the seed of David"; that speaks of the humanity of Jesus. "Remember Jesus Christ . . . raised from the dead"; that proclaims His deity.

When a Christian gets into difficulty, he needs to remember Christ's sympathetic understanding and divine power. There is no excuse for misunderstanding who Christ is.

In the Old Testament, when the Prophet Habakkuk was discouraged, he had to step back and consider God. Habakkuk had a real problem because Israel needed spiritual revival; and God's answer was to send judgment through the Chaldeans. Habakkuk was confused and angry. How could God use an ungodly nation to punish His people? Habakkuk thought he had God in a box, but God reaffirmed His plan and Habakkuk had to back off the problem and see himself in the right perspective. He told the Lord, in effect, that he didn't understand the problem or even how the Lord was dealing with it, but that he knew God was holy, and Habakkuk reaffirmed his trust in God. (See Hab. 1:12-13; 3:18-19.)

That is the way to solve every problem. The Christian must forget the problem and remember who Jesus Christ is and what He came to do. Remember who is in you. There is no place for fearful, lukewarm believers. Do we really know our resources? Have we considered the greatness of God's plan and our place in it? Truly, every believer needs a spirit of wisdom and revelation in the knowledge of God's plan.

PRACTICING YOUR POSITION

In Christ we are perfect positionally; but in practice we fall short. The Christian life is the experience of becoming in practice what we are in position. For every positional truth in the New Testament there is a corresponding practice we are to follow.

POSITION	PRACTICE
2 Peter 1:3-4	2 Peter 1:5-8
Eph. 1:3	Eph. 4:1
Col. 2:10	2 Tim. 3:17
Heb. 10:14	Col. 4:12
	Heb. 13:20-21
Spiritually alive	*Live the life*
Eph. 2:1, 4-5	Phil. 1:21
1 John 4:9	Gal. 2:20
John 11:25	Rom. 6:11-13
14:19	Titus 2:12
Acts 17:28	
Dead to sin	*Don't give in to sin*
Eph. 1:7	Rom. 6:11-15
1 John 1:9	Col. 3:3
2:12	
Rom. 6:2-10	
Forgiven	*Count on it!*
Eph. 1:7	Rom. 8:1, 33-34
1 John 1:9	
2:12	
Col. 1:14	
Made Righteous	*Live righteously*
Rom. 1:17	2 Tim. 2:22
3:21-26	1 John 3:7
4:1, 3, 6	
5:17	

Children of God	*Act like God's children*
Eph. 1:5	Eph. 5:1
Gal. 3:26	1 Peter 1:13-14
God's possession	*Yield to God*
Eph. 1:4	Rom. 12:1
2 Tim. 2:19	2 Tim. 2:19-21
Heirs of God	*Add to your inheritance*
Rom. 8:17	Matt. 6:19-21
Col. 1:12	2 Cor. 5:9-10
Eph. 1:11, 14, 18	2 John 8
1 Peter 1:3-4	1 Cor. 3:12-14
Blessed with all spiritual blessings in the heavenlies	*Cherish those blessings*
Eph. 1:3	Col. 3:1-2
2:6-7	
1 Peter 1:3-4	
Heavenly citizenship (Not of this world)	*Live as citizens of heaven*
Phil. 3:20	1 John 2:15
John 17:14-16	Col. 3:1-2
1 John 5:4-5	James 1:27
Servant of God	*Act like a servant*
1 Cor. 7:22-23	Rom. 6:17-19
Rom. 6:22	12:11
	Heb. 12:28
New life	*Walk in new life*
2 Cor. 5:17	Rom. 6:4
Free from law	*Yet keep fulfilling the law*
Rom. 6:14	Gal. 5:1
7:1-6	Rom. 8:4
Crucified to the world	*Avoid worldly things*
Gal. 1:4	1 John 2:15-17
6:14-15	James 4:4
	Rom. 12:2
Light to the world	*Walk as children of light*
1 Thes. 5:5	Eph. 5:8
Matt. 5:14	Matt. 5:15-16

Victorious over Satan	*Claiming victory*
Rev. 12:9-11	Eph. 6:11-17
	James 4:7
Cleansed	*Cleanse yourself*
John 15:3	2 Cor. 7:1
1 John 1:7, 9	Phil. 4:8
Holy and without blame	*Live holy lives*
Eph. 1:4	1 John 3:7
1 Cor. 3:17	1 Peter 1:15-16
	2 Peter 3:14
Free	*Enjoy your freedom*
John 8:32	Gal. 5:1
In Christ	*Abide in Him*
Eph. 1:3, 10	1 John 2:28
2:6, 13	
Secure in Christ	*Enjoy your security*
1 Peter 1:5	2 Peter 1:10
Rom. 8	
John 10:27-28	
Possessors of peace	*Let it rule*
Rom. 5:1	Rom. 14:19
14:17	Col. 3:15
John 14:27	
Acts 10:36	
One	*Live that oneness*
Eph. 4:4-6	Eph. 4:3
1:9-10	John 17:21
1 Cor. 12:13	
In grace	*Grow in grace*
Rom. 6:1	2 Peter 3:18
In fellowship	*Experience that fellowship*
1 John 1:3-7	1 Cor. 10:20
	Eph. 5:11
Joyful	*Experience that joy*
Rom. 5:2	1 John 1:4
	John 15:11
	16:24
	Phil. 4:4

Spirit indwelt and led	*Yield to the Spirit's control*
1 Cor. 6:19-20	Eph. 5:18
Rom. 8:9, 14	4:30
	1 Thes. 5:19
	Gal. 5:25
Spirit-gifted	*Use your gift*
1 Cor. 12:4	Rom. 12:3-6
Rom. 12:5-6	1 Peter 4:11
Empowered for service	*Claim and demonstrate that power*
Acts 1:8	1 Cor. 2:4
Eph. 3:20	Phil. 3:10
2 Cor. 4:7	Eph. 6:10
2 Tim. 1:7	Phil. 4:13
Love	*Love!*
Rom. 5:5	1 Peter 1:22
1 John 2:5	4:8
5:1	John 13:34-35
	1 John 3:18

4
SALVATION: ENTRANCE TO THE BODY

(Ephesians 2:1-10)

A young, handsome Muslim from India waited to talk with me after I had addressed a group of Hollywood movie people and invited those desiring to receive Christ as personal Saviour to see me afterward. When I told him how to trust in Jesus for salvation, he prayed and committed his life to Christ. Then he stood up, shook my hand, and said, "Isn't it wonderful! Now I have two gods—Jesus and Muhammad."

He thought he could choose several options. I explained his error. But his confusion was no worse than that of many Americans when it comes to understanding what a Christian really is. Some will say a person who lives in America, or who loves his mother, or who goes to church, or believes in God and is basically a good, moral type. Because of this confusion, we must analyze how the Scriptures define a Christian. As clearly as anywhere in the Bible, we find such a description in Ephesians. We've seen that the epistle first tells how all Christians constitute the Church, the Body of Christ. We've considered what it means to be in the Body, when it was formed, and what our resources are as members of that Body. At this point in his letter to the Ephesians, the Apostle Paul pauses to review how we came into the Body. There is one way—Jesus Christ. Paul reveals six facts necessary to a clear understanding of salvation (Eph. 2:1-10). We see that we are saved (1) from sin (2) by love (3) into life (4) with purpose (5) through faith (6) unto good works.

Salvation Is From Sin

I talk to people who say they believe in Jesus, but they have not turned from sin. There is no saved man who has not turned from sin. This does not mean he becomes sinless, but his life pattern has changed from a pursuit of sinfulness to pursuing godliness. It must be that way, for the Scripture says, "If any man be in Christ, he is a new creature: old things are passed away; behold, all things are become new" (2 Cor. 5:17).

Man's sinful state and practice are described first. "And you . . . who were dead in trespasses and sins; wherein in time past ye walked according to the course of this world, according to the prince of the power of the air, the spirit that now worketh in the children of disobedience: Among whom also we all had our conversation in times past in the lusts of our flesh, fulfilling the desires of the flesh and of the mind: and were by nature the children of wrath, even as others" (Eph. 2:1-3).

The natural man comes into the world spiritually dead. He is alienated from the life of God. Man's basic problem is not being out of harmony with his fellowmen, but being alienated from God.

I visited a home where a baby had died a half-hour earlier. The body was still warm. No stronger stimulus exists in humanity than that between a mother and her baby, but no matter how hard she tried that mother could not revive her baby. Death means total inability to respond, whatever the stimulus. That is how man is born into this world, spiritually; he cannot react to the stimulus of divine truth because the inner man is dead. He cannot sense the impulses of the divine world; he cannot feel the heartbeat of spiritual reality.

The natural man might sit in a church wondering what other people get out of it. He may read the Bible and say, "Man, that's strange stuff! I don't understand it at all." A

Christian tells about living for the glory of God instead of for self, and the natural man responds with, "You've given up everything that's really fun in life!"

One day as some men talked about following Jesus, one said, "'Lord, suffer me first to go and bury my father.' But Jesus said unto him, 'Follow Me; and let the dead bury their dead'" (Matt. 8:21-22).

Jesus' response brought to light physical and spiritual death. This potential disciple wanted to put off following Christ until his father died, because then he could cash in on the inheritance. His father was still living. But Jesus replied, in effect, "Let the spiritually dead bury the physically dead." In other words, let unbelievers take care of such things, and give yourself to the matters of the kingdom of God. There are two kinds of death: death of the body which we know as physical death, and death of the inner man which is spiritual death. When we are born, we are spiritually dead.

Paul defines spiritual death as an active condition: "in trespasses and sins." Man is spiritually dead not "because of" sin but "in" sin. Man is not a sinner because he sins; he sins because he is born sinful. So, besides man's inner spiritual deadness—his insensibility to spiritual impulses from God— he is involved in sinning.

Two words describe man's sinful condition. The Greek word for sin is *hamartia,* which literally means "to miss the mark." You shoot an arrow at a target and it falls short. The mark, of course, is God's perfect standard of righteousness (Matt. 5:48). Everyone fails to reach it. "For all have sinned, and come short of the glory of God" (Rom. 3:23).

Many persons have a false concept of sin. They think of murder, robbery, rape, and drunkenness as sin, but they don't think of the average "good guy" as a sinner. Sin is not necessarily violent, but is a failure to come up to the standard. A man may reach the mark of human goodness often; but since he cannot reach the mark of God's perfect holiness, he is still a sinner.

It's easy to confuse human goodness with the godly kind. Jesus said, "If ye do good to them which do good to you, what thank have ye? For sinners also do even the same" (Luke 6:33). There's a sense in which sinners do good to each other, if others do good to them. That's human, civic good. Shipwrecked at Malta, Luke noted, "The barbarous people showed us no little kindness" (Acts 28:2). People motivated by human goodness donate their blood, food, and money for charitable purposes. But civic, humanitarian goodness cannot compare with God's spiritual goodness. The Scriptures say, "There is none righteous, no, not one; there is none that understandeth, there is none that seeketh after God. They are all gone out of the way, they are together become unprofitable; there is none that doeth good, no, not one" (Rom. 3:10-12). The "good" referred to here is godly good. The best a natural man can do is human good.

The second word Paul uses to describe man's spiritual condition is *paraptoma* ("trespasses"). It once meant a slip or a fall, but came to mean traveling on the wrong road—going other than God's way. God says, "This is the way," but man says, "Sorry, I'm going to do my own thing." Man not only falls short *(hamartia)*, he also goes in the wrong direction *(paraptoma)*. Man tries but misses and goes his own way. "There is a way which seemeth right unto a man, but the end thereof are the ways of death" (Prov. 14:12).

The unsaved person is dead in trespasses and sins and as such he can't feel godly impulses, and doesn't understand divine truth. Often the only thing left is to follow the appeals of the world and the flesh. He will fall victim to whatever is around him. Though his spirit is insensitive, his body remains sensitive and he becomes the victim of bodily desires.

The first characteristic of this kind of life is that it is lived "according to the course of this world." An unsaved person does whatever the world is doing. Whatever the world is promoting, he is buying. He indulges in the sins of the times. He is at home and in complete harmony with the spirit of the age. There is always a spirit, an attitude, an influence pervading the world, and unsaved people are captured by it.

The world system today, as I see it, is selling humanism.

Humanism says man is the ultimate end of everything: he is captain of his soul, master of his fate. Yet man can't figure out how to solve the tensions between parents and teenagers, between parents themselves, between workers and managers, between nations. Instead, man appears the victim of everything that's gone wrong: decaying cities, spiraling crime and divorce, air and water pollution, hunger and poverty, population explosion, and wars and threats of wars. Mankind is simply incapable of solving problems alone.

According to humanism, it's all right for everyone to do his own thing. The truth is, man at no time has done so. Why not? "In time past ye walked according to the course of this world, according to the prince of the power of the air" (Eph. 2:2). A person's life is controlled either by God or by Satan. When a man rebels against God and disobeys Him, he is not a free man; he is a slave to the prince of demons himself.

The word for "prince" in Greek is *archon,* which means the first one in order, the highest in rank. Satan is the leader of a band of demons that inhabits the lower atmosphere. Scripture suggests there are three "heavens": the atmosphere around the earth, the stellar heavens, and the "heaven of heavens" where we'll abide with God. In the lower atmosphere encircling the earth a body of demons is activated and energized by Satan to corrupt men. "For we wrestle not against flesh and blood, but against principalities, against powers, against the rulers of the darkness of this world, against spiritual wickedness in high places" (6:12). The battle is not with men only, but with the prince of demons and his host of underlings.

Satan is active in the lives of unsaved people, energizing them to act on his behalf in his rebellion against God. Even an occasional good deed may be prompted by Satan to pacify a man's conscience so he will think he's really all right. People are dupes in Satan's war against God. The devil is a "roaring lion" (1 Peter 5:8), devouring people and using them to fight against God's power and against godly principles in the world.

A second characteristic of the spiritually dead is that they are "sons of disobedience." Children, without being taught, know how to disobey parents. In this life, then, a person constantly resists carrying out God's commands because what God tells him to do, Satan tells him not to do. For example, the Bible instructs a child, "Obey your parents," but Satan says, "Disobey." God tells husbands to love their wives, but Satan says, "Cheat on them; be unfaithful." The Bible tells wives to obey their husbands, but Satan tells them that's demeaning and old-fashioned. For everything God says, Satan shouts the opposite through the system.

The third characteristic of the spiritually dead is that they live to fulfill physical desires selfishly. The Apostle Paul indicts Jews and Gentiles alike. The Gentiles (which most of the Ephesian Christians were) are the "ye" of verse 2, and the Jews are the "we" of verse 3. The raw paganism and immorality of the Gentiles and the hypocritical self-righteousness of the Jews are all called "the lusts of the flesh." The unsaved man is left to fleshly desires because his spirit does not receive godly impulses. Spiritually dead persons gain satisfaction from fulfilling such desires; for many, it is all they get out of their living death.

The Greek word *thelema* is translated "desires" and can mean the irrational or forbidden. It suggests desire beyond the point of reason, beyond comprehension. It is marked by strong will. The outworking of *thelema* is described by Paul as "adultery [sexual infidelity in marriage], fornication [other kinds of sexual immorality], uncleanness [impurity, a dirty mind], lasciviousness [unrestrained abandonment to orgy], idolatry [worshiping false gods], witchcraft [dabbling in the occult], hatred, variance, emulations, wrath, strife, seditions, heresies [strife, jealousy, bad temper, selfishness, dissension, party spirit], envyings, murders, drunkenness, revellings" (Gal. 5:19-21). These are a catalog of what we see in human society today. It's because without God the inner man is spiritually dead.

The fourth trait of unregenerate man is that he is a child of "wrath." That means he is the object of God's judgment. Take a man who is dead in trespasses and sin, who follows the course of this world, who does what Satan wants, and fulfills the desires of the flesh, and you have a man who is dead center on the target of God's judgment. "The wrath of God is revealed from heaven against all ungodliness and unrighteousness of men" (Rom. 1:18).

Salvation, then, is deliverance from sin—from both the state and practice of sinfulness.

Salvation Is by Love

Man certainly is not lovable by virtue of his deeds and attitudes, but it requires love to reach man in his condition. His hopelessness can only be remedied if God intervenes. His intervention is reflected in the words, "But God. . . ." The picture of mankind is dismal indeed, but it changes. The ray of hope we see for ourselves is God's breaking in with His love. "But God, who is rich in mercy, for His great love wherewith He loved us" (Eph. 2:4). It is staggering to contemplate that in view of our condition, God would still love us. But His love does not depend on how good we are. It is His character to love.

God's love is shown in the richness of His mercy. Man needs nothing so much as mercy. If he got what he deserves, he would quickly be judged guilty, without hope. Instead it's as if God came into court and said, "You're guilty, but you may go free." If you asked Him why, He would say, "Because I love you." On the other hand, God is also just. Does He discard His justice in this case? No, it is for this reason Jesus had to die for sinners; He met the terms of justice so the sinner could have mercy. Someone had to die, because the just penalty for sin is death. Once the justice of God was satisfied in Christ, God could extend His mercy to sinful man.

Perhaps we should think of mercy and grace as two sides of God's love. Mercy means not giving us what we deserve. Grace is giving us what we don't deserve. Mercy holds back judgment; grace gives pardon. In His mercy God says, "I'll hold back judgment." In His grace God says, "I'll give you salvation." Mercy withholds God's wrath; grace releases His forgiveness. Mercy pities us, grace pardons us. Only love can prompt mercy and grace.

When my son Matt was disobedient, I would say, "Matt, I have to spank you." At this, his lip would quiver, he would reach to put his hands on my face, and say, "Dad, I love you." My first reaction was to say, "Don't confuse the issue. I know you love me." But when he said, "O Dad, I love you so much!" the punishment he deserved went out the window. I gave him a hug and a kiss and said, "Try to shape up, will you?" It's honest, genuine love that breeds mercy.

We can measure His love by the Cross. If we were to ask God to define His love, He might say this: "Do you see that rocky ridge outside Jerusalem? Do you see three crosses? My Son died on the one in the middle. That's how much I love you." Man's sin is not so much a crime against God's law as against His love. There is a difference. Someone has illustrated it this way:

Suppose I drive down the street, run a red light, and hit and kill a little boy. I'm charged with going through the red light and for manslaughter. I pay everything I owe to the state in terms of fines and imprisonment. It has no further claim on me. But it's another matter to be made right in my relationship with the mother. I committed a crime against love, not just against the law. A sentence satisfies the law; only the wronged person's forgiveness can satisfy a crime against love. There's no price tag on that. For my crime against love I'm at the mercy of the person I've wronged. I must wait until that mother freely forgives me.

We break God's law and sin against His love throughout our lives. The only way we become right with Him is when God says, "I forgive you." Our salvation is the act of His forgiveness, because He loves us.

Salvation Is into Life

Christ comes in and makes the spiritually dead person alive and sensitive to God. "Even when we were dead in sins, [God] quickened us together with Christ" (Eph. 2:5). The Word of God begins to speak to us. Christian love has meaning, and so does fellowship with other believers. We start to look at the world in a different light.

Man needs spiritual life, and Jesus says, "I'll give you that life, because I am that life." (See John 14:6.) Being alive "together with Christ" means a person is identified in Christ's death and resurrection. Paul said, "I am crucified with Christ: nevertheless I live" (Gal. 2:20). His death became mine when I received Christ, and I rose in newness of life. Because I identified myself with Him, my old life was put to death; because of His resurrection, I live.

Every Christian is totally identified with Christ. His life is not his own; Christ lives in him. He is no longer held in bondage by the desires of the flesh. He breaks out of the encirclement of sin and basks in Christ's freedom. That's what being spiritually alive means.

Salvation Has a Purpose

God had a purpose in mind when He planned salvation: "That in the ages to come He might show the exceeding riches of His grace in His kindness toward us through Christ Jesus" (Eph. 2:7). The believer died with Christ, rose with Him, and now lives a new kind of life. He actually sits together with Christ in the heavenlies; that is the new sphere of his spiritual existence. "For our citizenship is in heaven" (Phil. 3:20, NASB). The Christian is living eternal life right now; he lives forever in a world where God is real and Christ exists.

Beyond that, the believer's future is secure because of what God has done for him in Christ. Paul uses the past tense: "And hath raised us up together, and made us sit together in heavenly places in Christ Jesus" (Eph. 2:6). The Greek language has a unique feature. When the Greeks wanted to speak of things that were secure, they used the past tense. When they wanted to talk about something that couldn't change, that was inevitable, they expressed it as if it had already happened. The Christian's place in heaven is secure because God guaranteed it.

It is God's purpose that Christians be His great trophies of grace, displayed before all the angels for eternity. God's glory, grace, love, and mercy are seen nowhere as great as in the lives of those He has redeemed. When we look at what we were before our conversions (2:1-3), we understand why we are the greatest expression of His grace. We were at the bottom, but God gathered us up and placed us in heaven, so the angels might marvel and praise Him for what He did in His redemptive plan (3:10).

Everything exists for God's glory; thus He puts us on display. God receives the glory for what He has done in us. Someday, when we go bodily to heaven, we will show the host of heaven for eternity that God truly deserves glory.

> After this I beheld, and lo, a great multitude, which no man could number, of all nations, and kindreds, and people, and tongues, stood before the throne, and before the Lamb, clothed with white robes, and palms in their hands; and cried with a loud voice, saying, "Salvation to our God which sitteth upon the throne, and unto the Lamb." And all the angels stood round about the throne . . . and fell before the throne on their faces, and worshiped God, saying, "Amen: Blessing, and glory, and wisdom, and thanksgiving, and honor, and power, and might, be unto our God for ever and ever. Amen (Rev. 7:9-12).

Why were angels praising God? Because of His redemptive work. These people were the trophies of His grace, and they glorified God so much that the host of heaven broke out into joyful praise. Considering where we came from and what we will be, we ought never to stop thanking God for His wisdom, mercy, and love.

Salvation Is through Faith

Saving faith is the gift of God. God gave us His love, mercy, and grace, and then the faith to respond. Faith in itself is not a human work that earns salvation: salvation is "not of works," not even of faith as a work. God *gives* faith. If faith were of ourselves, we could say, "See, I had sense enough to put my faith in God." But, no, that would be boasting of works. Paul concludes that God gives us faith along with everything else (see Phil. 1:29). The spiritual realm opens to the dead natural man only when God in sovereign grace by a creative act opens the spiritual understanding. By faith, man responds to this act. This is spiritual rebirth. By the miracle of regeneration a dead man becomes alive to the spiritual dimension and enters the mainstream of the life of God.

The spiritual truth may be illustrated by human birth. When a baby is born, the doctor slaps his bottom and he begins to breathe. He breathes on his own. Smart baby! Baby knows if he's going to stay alive he has to breathe. No, the truth is, he breathes because he was whacked and felt pain. He instinctively cried. Why does a person breathe spiritually through faith? Because God, as it were, slaps him with divine grace. Faith is merely a response to the grace of God, which jolts someone into spiritual life.

Thus the Bible speaks of conversion as a new birth from above (John 3:3-8). New birth is a gift, which may not be earned. A baby can't bring itself into life. The same is true with spiritual life; God brings it into existence. All man does is to believe it exists through Christ and to claim it.

Salvation Is unto Good Works

Salvation is not by human works such as confirmation, baptism, church membership, church attendance, Communion, keeping the Ten Commandments, living by the Sermon on the Mount, giving to charity, or being a good neighbor. Doing one or all of these things will not bring us from spiritual death to life. However, once a person is reborn by faith in Christ, his life is to be characterized by good works. We are saved "unto" good works, not "by" them.

A Christian is born to produce good works. He is God's "workmanship" (Eph. 2:10), a word which in Greek may mean "masterpiece." As God's masterpiece, the Christian is to continue doing good works. God gives the believer new life in Christ; daily He is molding him into Christ's likeness.

A Sunday School teacher explaining Creation was irritated

by one boy in the class. Thinking to shock the pupil, the teacher asked, "Who made you?"

"God did," the boy replied.

"Well, He didn't do a very good job!"

The boy retorted, "That's 'cause He ain't finished with me yet!"

In a practical sense, the boy was right.

The outworking for the believer is to walk in the good works that God has "ordained" for him. He is saved "unto" good works; now he is to do them. This is part of his salvation; it produces good works now. God has equipped His people to carry out His plan, which begins with the gift of faith and continues in the lifelong process of entering into good works. The Apostle John tells us the end of this process. "Beloved, now are we the sons of God, and it doth not yet appear what we shall be: but we know that, when He [Christ] shall appear, we shall be like Him; for we shall see Him as He is" (1 John 3:2).

"We shall be like Him" because God saved us from sin and death, giving us the life of Christ. He acts in love, gives us faith to respond to that love, designs good works for us to walk in, and plans to display us before angels. Such is the scope of salvation.

5
RELEASING POWER IN THE BODY

(Ephesians 3:14-21)

Christian experience is a matter of applying God's power to the needs of everyday living. But many times Christians are frustrated because they don't know how to activate God's power.

My car has a lot of power under the hood. But I must have the key, put it into the ignition switch, and turn it on, or none of that horsepower will do anything. If I know how every part of my car operates, and if every part is in perfect working order, I may say to my car, "Take me to the store," and it won't move. I have to use the key to turn on the power.

Paul prayed that Christians know how to ignite God's power (Eph. 3:14-21). The prayer outlines five aspects of the power available to those in the Body: (1) inner strength; (2) the indwelling Christ; (3) incomprehensible love; (4) infinite fullness; (5) release of power. From this prayer we learn how to use God's power in our lives.

Inner Strength
The first key to using the power is inner strength. But for the proper setting, we must connect 3:1 to 3:14. The intervening verses are a kind of parenthetical aside in Paul's thought. "For this cause I Paul, the prisoner of Jesus Christ for you Gentiles . . . For this cause I bow my knees unto the Father of

our Lord Jesus Christ" (3:1, 14). Paul repeats himself to show he is resuming his train of thought. Then he reviews the truths of God's plan and goes on to worship God as well as to pray for the Church.

Paul is driven to his knees by the sheer realization of all the resources he has in God's plan. He describes God as the Father "of whom the whole family in heaven and earth is named" (3:15). One Body, one Family, God's Family is the emphasis in Ephesians. The Church comprises God's Family because believers are His children. All believers "have access by one Spirit unto the Father" (2:18); all comprise "the Household of God" (2:19).

Paul is about to make a request, but he prefaces his request by acknowledging God as his Father. When a believer goes to God, he does not approach Him in the spirit of fear; instead he cries, "Abba, Father," because he knows the Father loves him. He comes to prayer with boldness and confidence. Paul prays that God will grant his request "according to the riches of His glory" (3:16). He asks that all God's attributes, all the depth of His glory, be at the disposal of the Christian. If a rich man gives you something out of his riches, it may be 25¢; but if he gives you something according to his riches, it will be to the outer limits of his wealth. God always gives that way. Salvation is "according to the riches of His grace" (1:7). Paul believed that God would supply all his needs "according to His riches in glory" (Phil. 4:19). A person's problem may be very serious, seemingly insoluble, but God's riches are infinitely available to him. In Christ they are "unsearchable" (Eph. 3:8).

On the basis of this wealth at his disposal, Paul prays for strength "in the inner man" (3:16). How does it work? As the Christian yields his life day by day to the Holy Spirit, he gains strength within.

The Christian critically needs inner strength today in view of the unique emotional and physical pressures that tear at him, knocking him off balance, leading him to despair, discouragement, and hopelessness. A weak inner man can't stand the pressure.

If the inner man is weak, sin takes over and the believer can't resist it. He may become frustrated, guilty, and out of balance emotionally, mentally, and spiritually. The mental strain may lead to physical illness.

However, it is possible for the Christian's inner man to be "strengthened with might" (3:16). Literally, this means "empowered with power." The supernatural power at the believer's disposal is so great that Paul uses two Greek words to describe it, *krataio* ("to make strong") and *dunamis* ("power"). Such is the dynamic power available to the inner man.

Since the Holy Spirit strengthens the inner man we must understand the filling of the Spirit. Though believers possess the Holy Spirit, some are weak inside. Filling occurs only as the believer yields to the Holy Spirit; yields his life completely to Him. It works like this:

Life consists of a host of decisions. If a person is filled with the Holy Spirit, he says, in effect, "I have to make a decision. Show me the way to go." If he sees a temptation coming, he allows the Holy Spirit to meet it and defeat Satan. The Spirit-filled life is living in Spirit-awareness.

This relationship is not complicated. It is taking a step at a time, allowing the Holy Spirit to be in charge. This relationship is developed by the discipline of regular Bible reading and prayer. God's Word reveals the mind of the Spirit and in prayer the believer commits himself daily to the Holy Spirit.

Being filled is similar to a hand with a glove. By itself a glove does nothing; but if I put my hand into it, the glove is under my control. The glove doesn't argue and resist; it moves under the control of my fingers. The glove's only strength is my hand. The Christian's strength is the Holy Spirit.

Paul could pray for believers to be strengthened internally, because God had done it for him. "My grace is sufficient for thee; for My strength is made perfect in weakness" (2 Cor. 12:9). Paul accepted this principle of divine working and rejoiced in it. He responded to God, "Most gladly therefore will I rather glory in my infirmities, that the power of Christ may rest upon me. Therefore I take pleasure in infirmities, in reproaches, in necessities, in persecutions, in distresses for Christ's sake: for when I am weak, then am I strong" (vv. 9-10).

How did this work out practically for Paul? When Paul left Ephesus for the last time, the Holy Spirit revealed that "bonds and afflictions" awaited him. Nevertheless, he went ahead resolving that "none of these things move me, neither count I my life dear unto myself, so that I might finish my course with joy, and the ministry, which I have received of the Lord Jesus, to testify the Gospel of the grace of God" (Acts 20:24).

He faced affliction confidently in the strength of the Holy Spirit, and later recounted it: "With far greater labors, far more imprisonments, with countless beatings, and often near death. Five times I have received at the hands of the Jews 40 lashes less one. Three times I have been beaten with rods; once I was stoned. Three times I have been shipwrecked; a night and a day I have been adrift at sea; on frequent journeys, in danger from rivers, danger from robbers, danger from my own people, danger from Gentiles, danger in the city, danger in the wilderness, danger at sea, danger from false brethren, in toil and hardship, through many a sleepless night, in hunger and thirst, often without food, in cold and exposure. And, apart from other things, there is the daily pressure upon me of my anxiety for all the churches" (2 Cor. 11:23-28, RSV).

What a catalog of experiences! Paul was not nervous and defeated. He was strong in the inner man, because he was filled by the Holy Spirit and allowed the Spirit to direct his life. Further testimony:

We are handicapped on all sides, but we are never frustrated; we are puzzled, but never in despair. We are persecuted, but we never have to stand it alone: we may be knocked down but we are never knocked out! Every day we experience something of the death of Jesus, so that we may also know the power of the life of Jesus in these bodies of ours. . . . This is the reason why we never collapse. The outward man does indeed suffer wear and tear, but every

day the inward man receives fresh strength
(2 Cor. 4:8-10, 16, PH).

Only in the Holy Spirit did Paul have that kind of power. The
first step to unleashing power in the Body is to lay hold of
inner strength by the Holy Spirit. If the Christian is weak inside,
nothing will happen.

The Indwelling Christ

As the inner man is strengthened by the Holy Spirit, Christ
dwells in his heart. Paul doesn't say Christ "comes into your
heart"—that is salvation. He says, "That Christ may dwell in
your hearts" (3:17). The difference is between coming initially
and dwelling thereafter. The distinction appears in the Greek
word used for "dwell," *katoikeo,* which means literally "to
settle down." It carries the idea of coming into a home and
settling down there. When a Christian is strong within, Christ,
who is already there, settles down and feels at home. A
believer must ask himself whether Jesus is comfortable in his
heart. When there is sin and disobedience, Christ is not at
home.

In his booklet, *My Heart Christ's Home,** Robert Munger
gives a simple but vivid illustration of this spiritual principle.
He compares his heart to a home. Since Christ has come
there to live, He asks to go through it. First He goes to the
library—the control room, the brain where all the thoughts
are, where information is stored. Jesus finds evil and untruth.
It has to go, so the man cleans it out. In the library there
should be a portrait of Jesus, a reminder that Jesus is at the
center of his consciousness.

Next is the dining room, the room of appetites and desires.
Jesus asks the man what he longs for. He wants leeks, garlic,
and onions—all the worldly delights. Jesus says, "If you want
food that really satisfies, seek the will of My Father."

When they enter the living room, Jesus says, "You know, I
sit in the living room every morning and you come right

---

*(InterVarsity Press, Downers Grove, Ill.)

through here so fast you never stop to talk to Me." The living room represents fellowship, conversation, sharing. Jesus says, "I've been a guest in your house, but you don't talk to Me."

In the workshop Jesus sees many toys the man has made with his tools. "Is that what you've done with your skills?" He asks. "Use your talents, your abilities for the kingdom of God." Jesus should control this room too.

Finally the man and his Saviour return upstairs, only to encounter a strange odor coming from the hall closet. It represents secret sins. The man is upset; he figures if Jesus controls the dining room, living room, library, and workshop, that should be enough. But the odor persists. Jesus asks him to open the closet door. The things he didn't want to turn over to Jesus have to come out.

Only when Jesus controls every room is He really at home in our hearts. This comes about by the indwelling Spirit. His work is to extend the lordship of Jesus Christ to every part of the believer's life. First we yield to the Holy Spirit. The result of being filled is strength in the inner man. As the inner man strengthens, Jesus cleanses the "heart home" and is at rest there. In wondrous condescension, He is willing to leave the infinite majesty of heaven and make His home in our hearts. Jesus said, "If a man love Me, he will keep My words: and My Father will love him, and We will come unto him, and make Our abode with him" (John 14:23).

Jesus wants to "settle down" in the life of each believer.

Incomprehensible Love

When Christ settles down in a believer's life, love grows everywhere. Using the metaphor of planting a tree, Paul says that when Christ dwells in our hearts we are "rooted and grounded in love." Jesus said, "A new commandment I give unto you, that ye love one another; as I have loved you, that ye also love one another. By this shall all men know that ye are My disciples, if ye have love one to another" (John 13:34-35).

If the world fails to recognize Christians, it's because

Christians lack love for one another. God loves the world and wants to demonstrate that love through Christians. That can happen only when the Christian yields himself to the Holy Spirit, is strong in the inner man, and allows Jesus to fill his life. Then love will burst forth, because it is Jesus' nature to love. He will show His love if He has an open channel.

Peter echoes these thoughts: "Who by Him do believe in God, that raised Him up from the dead, and gave Him glory; that your faith and hope might be in God. Seeing ye have purified your souls in obeying the truth through the Spirit unto unfeigned love of the brethren, see that ye love one another with a pure heart fervently" (1 Peter 1:21-22).

Before a Christian can love people fervently, he must be established in love. Before he can be established in love, he must have a pure heart. To have a pure heart he must resist temptation. To resist temptation he must be strong in the inner man. To be strong in the inner man he must be controlled by the Holy Spirit.

When we arrive at the Spirit-filled life, we are not at the end. It is the beginning. When Christ settles down in our lives, things happen. Love is the by-product of this spiritual process. "That ye . . . may be able to comprehend, with all saints, what is the breadth, and length, and depth, and height; and to know the love of Christ, which passeth knowledge" (Eph. 3:17-19).

The only way to comprehend the love of Christ is to be rooted and grounded in it. Someone asked Louis Armstrong about jazz, and the famous trumpeter said, "Man, if I got to explain it, you ain't got it." That's how it is with love. If a person has to tell you what it is, you don't have it.

If you are a parent, and someone tells you, "I really love my little child," you understand. But children don't always understand how much a parent can love, because they aren't parents.

"Comprehend" in Greek is *katalambano,* which means "to seize" something and make it one's own. The only way we can seize the love of Christ and comprehend it, is to be grounded in it.

Christ's love is so great it is expressed in four dimensions: breadth, length, depth, and height. An early Christian used the cross as the symbol of Christ's love. The post points upward and downward (height and depth), the crosspiece to the horizons (breadth and length).

The Letter to the Ephesians itself reveals the extent of Christ's love. The *breadth* of Christ's love reaches to the Jew on the one hand, Gentile on the other (2:16-18). It's *length* is eternity past to eternity future. He chose believers "before the foundation of the world . . . in love" (1:4).

Christ's love is so *deep* it reaches down into the pit of sin and spiritual death and pulls us out of it (2:1). The believer has been raised to sit with Jesus in heaven. He has been *lifted* from the pit to an exalted position in glory (2:6).

Can a Christian understand the dimensions of Christ's love when faced with what looks like a disastrous situation? If he can, he may be able to say to God, "I can't wait to see how You will show me Your love in this." In every circumstance the believer who comprehends Christ's love is able to say, "All right now, Lord, I've got a grasp of it."

Infinite Fullness
"Filled with all the fullness of God" (3:19). Perhaps we can imagine Paul getting excited about this truth before he actually wrote it in his letter.

Having the fullness of God means total spiritual richness. It doesn't mean that all there is of God comes to live in the believer; that can't be. God does not move into you and limit Himself to your capacity. It's like drawing a thimbleful of water from a lake. The thimble is filled with the lake, but you don't have the whole lake in the thimble. That thimble doesn't diminish the lake, yet it has the "fullness" of the lake in the sense that the thimble contains a particle of every ingredient of the water. All the essential character of that lake is in the thimble.

In the same way, when a believer has the fullness of God, he possesses the essential characteristics of God. But God is not diminished. The believer can communicate what God is like to the world. He radiates God out of that fullness.

Since God is love, a believer filled with the fullness of God will express godly love. Since God is wise, a believer filled with the fullness of God will express godly wisdom. Since God is holy, the believer filled with the fullness of God will display holiness. Since God is gracious, a believer filled with the fullness of God will communicate godly graciousness.

Those attributes God deposits in the Christian in reduced measure, so he can love with divine love, judge with divine wisdom, and live with divine holiness—without being divine himself. In a word, to be filled with all the fullness of God is to be godlike: wise, just, holy, pure, loving, gracious, merciful. We meet too few Christians who have this fullness but when we do, we recognize it. A person who radiates the fullness of God is attractive and powerful.

This whole concept obviously staggers the mind. How could God take a worthless human being, a rebel against His love, and give him His fullness? Our response should be "Thank You, God, for putting Your fullness in me. Thank You for helping me to radiate Your wonderful person."

If the world is to understand that God is love, love must be seen in Christians. If people are to recognize that God is wise, they must see God's wisdom in believers. Christians are responsible to communicate who God is by their lives.

Internal Power
Lest we think that in having the fullness of God we are at the summit, Paul now talks about unleashing God's power in our lives.

That power becomes available to him who is filled with God's fullness. Possessing God's power means that in the believer God can do things "abundantly above" what the believer asks or thinks. God "is able to do . . . according to the power . . . in us" (Eph. 3:20-21).

Paul explains what he means. "But we have this treasure in earthen vessels, that the excellency of the power may be of

God, and not of us" (2 Cor. 4:7). It is thrilling to see this power at work when we are aware of our own incapacities.

What is the answer for a Christian who feels his life is a fizzle? Consider again the progressive development of power in the Body of Christ. It starts with the inner man made strong by the Holy Spirit. Christ makes Himself at home in the believer, and as a result the believer comprehends love. Then he is filled with the fullness of God, and power is released in his life.

The goal of this spiritual development is the glory of God. Some Christians ask, "Why bother with all this? I'm going to heaven anyway." God wants to be glorified in the Church *now* (Eph. 3:21). Every Christian should be able to say "Amen" to Paul's prayer, and in that way say, "Let it be so in my life."

6
HIGH POSITION DEMANDS A LOWLY WALK

(Ephesians 4:1-6)

When a person joins an organization, he obligates himself to live by its rules and standards. He gives himself to its goals and he is expected to conform to what the organization stands for.

In the Body of Christ conformity is expected also. As a believer joins God's Family, he belongs to his heavenly Father. He shows that he shares the goals of the Body and wants to conform to what God requires. This is a conformity of love. If a Christian fails to conform to the pattern of the Body, it's not because he lacks rules; rather he lacks love, for love fulfills the Law (see Rom. 13:10).

When the Christian enters the Body, he receives rights, privileges, and honors (Eph. 1—3), and he is expected to act like a member of the Body.

When a person knows the truth, the obvious thing for him is to show it. Duty is the obvious response to doctrine. It is not a random response, but the only proper one. Paul turns to writing about behavior with a "Therefore" (Eph. 4:1) as the link between the chapters on doctrine and duty. Paul also makes this connection in Romans (12:1) after 11 chapters of doctrine, and also in Galatians (5:1) after 4 chapters of doctrine.

71

The Body needs consistent doctrinal teaching. Teaching duty without doctrine weakens the counsel of God for the believer. It leads to a legalistic spirit or causes the believer to try to rely on emotional pep talks. Without doctrine, the believer lacks the true motive for Christian living. He needs the solid facts of the Word of God rather than human appeals to duty.

In the New Testament are numerous references to the need for knowing sound doctrine. We read that the Christian is "renewed in knowledge" (Col. 3:10), that we are to "grow in grace, and in the knowledge of our Lord and Saviour Jesus Christ" (2 Peter 3:18), and that knowledge is the key to good works (Col. 1:10). The basis of a solid spiritual foundation is knowledge.

Conduct Is Related to Knowledge

A Christian's conduct is directly related to the extent of his knowledge. He may limp along because he is ignorant doctrinally. He may never dig into the Word of God. Then he may hear of a painless cure to his problem, something that usually involves an emotional charge, and he goes after a new feeling rather than sound doctrinal knowledge. The results are superficial. That is why Paul has been careful to delineate basic doctrine. The transfer from doctrine to duty is a key New Testament concept; they are inseparably linked. "Put on therefore, as the elect of God, holy and beloved, bowels of mercies, kindness, humbleness of mind, meekness, long-suffering" (3:12). "If ye then be risen with Christ, seek those things which are above. . . . Set your affection on things above, not on things on the earth" (3:1-2).

The believer's position is "risen with Christ." If that's true, he is supposed to behave in a certain manner. Duty follows position. Except for God Himself, no one is in a more exalted position than the Christian. The believer himself had nothing to do with his position; it is all of God. The true Christian response to a high position is humility. The believer's high position demands a lowly walk.

The Call to the Worthy Walk

Paul himself is one who walked worthy of his calling, no matter what the price. He had been faithful to his trust; he had fulfilled his calling. It led to a Roman prison yet he was loyal to his Lord.

But Paul was also passionately concerned for the spiritual welfare of those whom he had been called to serve. The depth of his concern is revealed in the words, "I . . . beseech you" (Eph. 4:1). The Christian's *vocation* in this verse is not his job, his profession, or his career, but his calling to salvation, to the Body of Christ. Paul's appeal for a worthy walk is rooted in his status as a prisoner *in* Rome as he writes this letter. However, he never considered himself a prisoner *of* Rome, but a prisoner of the Lord. His bondage was in the plan of God. Paul was confident that God, not the Roman government, was in control of his life. Once he had been imprisoned in Philippi, and at that time God saw fit to deliver him. If God wanted him set free from the Romans, He could deliver him.

But how is Paul's appeal rooted in imprisonment? This way: He believed we should be loyal to our calling in Christ no matter what. Paul was saying, in effect, "Look, friends, I'm a prisoner. That's about as bad off as one can get, and I can still say, 'Walk worthy of your calling.' It may lead to jail, but don't consider that the important thing."

Why did Paul care so much? Because his purpose in life was to "present every man perfect in Christ Jesus" (Col. 1:28). He could not settle for less than total spiritual maturity in every believer to whom he ministered. Paul simply begged people to live out their Christian commitments. It was the passion of his life. And he was expendable in that effort.

Paul's burden should be the burden of every pastor. If he doesn't yearn for the spiritual growth of his people and exhort his people toward spiritual maturity, he should leave the ministry. Epaphras was one who labored fervently that believers would "stand perfect and complete in all the will of God" (4:12).

The word *walk* (Eph. 4:1) describes the Christian's daily

conduct, his lifestyle. This idea is seen repeatedly in the New Testament: "That ye would walk worthy of God, who hath called you unto His kingdom and glory" (1 Thes. 2:12), "Let your conversation [conduct] be as it becometh the Gospel of Christ" (Phil. 1:27), "That ye might walk worthy of the Lord unto all pleasing, being fruitful in every good work, and increasing in the knowledge of God" (Col. 1:10).

Perhaps the best explanation of the need to walk worthy is found in a phrase Paul uses in his letter to Titus: "That they may adorn the doctrine of God our Saviour in all things" (2:10). Because the Christian's calling is "high" (Phil. 3:14), "holy" (2 Tim. 1:9), and "heavenly" (Heb. 3:1), he is supposed to live by a certain standard of conduct. A godly life brings to light before men the various facets of God's transforming grace and love. A life of obedience to God, of holiness, humility, love, joy, and peace shines like so many precious jewels, adorning the truth.

Suppose, for example, you try to explain to an unbeliever the truth about God. He has doubts. Then one day he encounters, in a different way, a godly person. In addition to hearing intellectual truth, he sees it in action. Truth becomes attractive and appealing to him. That's how a Christian, by his worthy walk, can adorn the doctrine of God in the eyes of the world. This is a great responsibility, but we can fulfill it. The early Church multiplied according to its godly walk (Acts 9:31). If all believers today adorned the doctrine of God by godliness in their behavior, there would be a tremendous impact on the world.

Characteristics of the Worthy Walk

Having stressed the necessity of a worthy walk, Paul gives five characteristics of it: (1) lowliness; (2) meekness; (3) long-suffering; (4) forbearance; (5) unity (Eph. 4:2-3).

Lowliness is genuine humility that comes from an association with Jesus Christ. A Christian can know a lot of doctrine, memorize Bible verses, be faithful to the church, and be involved in many Christian activities, but not be walking in humility.

Pride is disastrous to Christian experience. In the Greek world Paul knew, humility was mocked. The word *tapeino-phrosune*, translated "lowliness" does not even appear in classical Greek; it was coined by Christians. The Christians introduced humility to the world of their time.

When a Christian looks for an example of humility, he need look only at Christ. "Let this mind be in you, which was also in Christ Jesus" (Phil. 2:5). Real discipleship begins here.

What Paul cited as a characteristic of the worthy walk, he himself exemplified. "Serving the Lord with all humility of mind, and with many tears, and temptations [trials], which befell me by the lying in wait of the Jews" (Acts 20:19). This was his farewell statement to the elders at Ephesus, so when he wrote to them later they could recall the example of his life before them. He was often ambushed by his enemies, so to speak, but he persevered with humility.

Humility comes from proper self-awareness. It comes hard because it begins only when we honestly face ourselves. Bernard said "humility is the virtue by which a man becomes conscious of his own unworthiness." However, many people waltz through life with their minds behind a facade, cultivating pride because they don't have the courage to look at themselves and see what they really are. A person has no reason to exalt himself.

Humility also results from Christ-awareness—measuring oneself by the divine standard. A person may think he rates high against mediocre standards. For example, when I was in high school I received a gold trophy as "player of the year"; when I got to college I found a lot of other top players. Next, I went to a pro football training camp, and there I saw that I was really nothing special by professional standards. In track I was good enough to win ribbons in my school but when I got into the finals of the county invitational meet, I won no medal. I was nothing compared to the big boys.

A Christian may look outstanding compared with the alcoholic who lives down the street. But godless neighbors are not the believer's standard; his standard is Jesus Christ. No matter how good a Christian thinks he is, when he compares himself with Jesus, he doesn't come anywhere near Him. This is the road to humility.

God-awareness is another factor in humility. It is realizing that if it weren't for God, we wouldn't exist. Humility is acknowledging that God controls everything. When a person becomes too proud, God often reaffirms His sovereign control in that life. That is humbling.

The worthy walk starts with *lowliness* and continues with *meekness.* Meekness is the attitude of a person who submits to God's dealings without regret and to man's wickedness without revenge. The meek person doesn't continually insist on his rights; he would rather take the wrong than inflict it on someone else.

This does not mean he is a wishy-washy, spineless person. He has true character and backbone. It takes more strength to be meek than to fight for rights. The meek person has courage and convictions. As Aristotle said, he is angry at the right time and not angry at the wrong time. If he's angry, it's because God is maligned, not because he himself has been hurt. He is concerned about the sufferings of others, but he doesn't get upset when he suffers.

Yet some Christians act like children, insisting on their rights all the time. If they are offended, they take their ball and go home. "I'm never going back to that church," they declare. When someone offends us we have opportunity to learn meekness.

As He exemplified humility, so the Lord Jesus Christ also showed what meekness is (see 2 Cor. 10:1). When people rejected Him, He didn't become bitter; He "endured the cross, despising the shame" (Heb. 12:2). Despite the wicked treatment He suffered at the hands of men, Jesus prayed, "Father, forgive them; for they know not what they do" (Luke 23:34). Meekness requires the greatest amount of fortitude in time of crisis.

Meekness is really a spirit of submission. If it seems to be a downward step, remember how far down it was for Jesus. The One who made the world and sustains it became the meek and lowly One, and set the pattern for a worthy Christian walk.

Think what beauty and power would characterize the Body of Christ if meekness and lowliness were the order of the day, with no one insisting on his own rights.

The third component of a worthy walk is *long-suffering.* No matter how bad life gets, the long-suffering person keeps plugging away. Specifically, the word in Greek, *makrothumia,* means taking whatever men dish out, bearing insult, injury, and complaint with patient endurance, without bitterness and irritation. The long-suffering Christian loves and waits.

The Body of Christ needs this virtue. It often is fractured when a believer is offended and makes a big issue of it. Instead, he should endure the offense, remember the worthy walk, and press on as Jesus did. The Christian is not called to retaliate (see 1 Cor. 6:7).

Paul describes the fourth characteristic of the worthy walk as *forbearing one another* in love (Eph. 4:2). This is the outworking of the first three. Forbearing one another means loving one another, even though the other might offend. The Christian has room in his love to accommodate others' mistakes.

The forbearing believer says with patient love, "I know you didn't mean it. You shouldn't have acted like that, but I love you." This kind of spirit instantly heals breaches in the fellowship of the Body. Whenever there is a problem in the Body, apply the salve of forbearance.

Jesus was forbearing in the face of slander, insult, and physical abuse. Jesus asks that the Christian who is wronged assume the same spirit He showed toward His persecutors. This attitude is described by Peter as "fervent charity . . . [which] shall cover the multitude of sins" (1 Peter 4:8). If I love only perfection, then I don't have Christian love. I must allow room for a brother to make a mistake, even toward me, and still love him.

When the four characteristics of the worthy walk are in motion, the fifth one follows: "Endeavoring to keep the unity of the Spirit in the bond of peace" (Eph. 4:3). Peace is the bond which maintains unity. Peace springs from love, love from humility. People can be at peace with each other because they love each other. The result of the worthy walk is unity.

The key to obtaining the fifth characteristic of the worthy walk is *endeavoring to keep.* We have to work at unity to keep it. "Endeavor" means putting forth an effort. Suppose we face some choices in a given situation. We decide one way and there's bound to be discord. Or we may decide another way that will lead to preserving unity in the Body. Which should we choose? The way that will keep unity.

It is important to note that Scripture does not command Christians to *create* unity. We are already one Body in Christ; we are to *keep* what we already have. We don't need church conferences on unity, but we do need to encourage one another to live the kind of life that is lowly, meek, long-suffering, and forbearing in love.

Acquiring these virtues in the Christian's worthy walk depends on death to self, on submission of the ego. So long as self is at the center of life, so long as personal feelings and prestige have top priority, the worthy walk is unreachable. If self is first, the doctrine of God is not adorned, a believer cannot be at peace with other believers, and the Body will not experience oneness.

Why a Worthy Walk?

In these verses unity emerges as the reason for the worthy walk. God planned unity from the beginning. Seven "unities" comprise the basis for the walk.

First God commands Christians to keep unity because there is *one Body* (Eph. 4:4). There are many local assemblies and congregations, but one Body. The Church is made up of believers of all ages, races, and nationalities. Though Christians differ in race, custom, culture, national origin, and language, and may be educated, uneducated, rich, or poor, they are one in Christ. Some are in heaven, some on earth, but all believers from Pentecost to the Rapture comprise Christ's Body.

The Body's unity transcends all human organizations. The

Body is not always seen as one outwardly; denominational distinctives tend to fragment the Body rather than unify it.

The unity of believers is intended to be a witness to the world. Jesus prayed for believers to express their oneness "that the world may believe that Thou hast sent Me" (John 17:21). This oneness is a sign that the Father loved the world and sent His Son into it (17:23). If the Church does not show true oneness, it appears to the world to be just another social organization with the same quarrels and divisions other groups have.

Along with emphasis on one Body is the clear teaching of one Spirit (Eph. 4:4). The Holy Spirit is the source of Christian unity, because He lives in every believer (Rom. 8:9) and He is within the Church collectively, as well as individually.

We see this truth in other parts of the epistle. "In whom ye also are built together for an habitation of God through the Spirit" (Eph. 2:22) and again, "Endeavoring to keep the unity of the Spirit" (4:3).

This unity is based on the fact that the Holy Spirit is the agent of the new birth (John 3:5-8), and consequently comes to indwell the believer (John 14:16-17; 1 Cor. 12:13).

Because of this we can test whether a work is of the Spirit. If division arises within the Body, we can be sure it is not of the Spirit. That is a very helpful test in this day, when there are many religious expressions claiming to be genuine.

This was the test applied in the Book of Acts. The Holy Spirit was the sign of spiritual validity. The question of whether the Gentiles had really been saved without keeping the Jewish law was debated at the Council of Jerusalem (Acts 15). Speaking of the converted Gentiles, Peter said, "God, which knoweth the hearts, bare them witness, giving them the Holy Spirit, even as He did unto us" (15:8). The same Spirit-induced phenomena of Pentecost accompanied the outreach of the Gospel to the Gentiles. At Pentecost the Holy Spirit came on the believing Jews at Jerusalem and later, when the Gospel went to the Gentiles, the Holy Spirit came on them in the same way (Acts 8:17).

God wanted the Jewish believers to know that when the Holy Spirit came on the Gentiles, He came in the same way as He did on them; thus the outward sign of His coming— tongues—was the same. The Jewish believers had to be sure the Gentiles had received the same Spirit. One part of the Body could not say to another part, "We have something you don't have." The Holy Spirit is the common denominator in the Body.

Believers share *one hope* too (Eph. 4:4), even though the circumstances of our calling to that hope are different. Each member of the Body is unique, but all share a common goal which is to be like Jesus Christ (Rom. 8:29).

There is no doubt about the believer's hope. It is not wishful thinking. It is certainty. The reason the believer may be sure of his hope is that the Holy Spirit has been given to him as down payment. God has given to the Christian "the earnest of the Spirit" (2 Cor. 5:5). That word "earnest" means "first installment," something like an engagement ring. The Holy Spirit is the guarantee in the believer that someday he will receive his inheritance.

One Spirit, One Lord

A proper concept of the Holy Spirit is crucial to understanding the believer's place in the body. The Holy Spirit places him in the Body, indwells him and is the guarantee of the future, the security of the Church's hope (Eph. 4:4).

Every Christian confesses and serves the same Lord Jesus Christ (4:5). He is Lord of all members of His Body, the living and the dead. Christians have a common Master, a common commitment and allegiance.

It is strange, then, that Christians sometimes follow different orders. The Body was not made to function that way. I remember one day at home I told my daughter, "Marcy, close the door." As she started toward it, my wife called, "Marcy, why are you closing the door? Leave it open!" Marcy was the victim of conflicting orders.

In the Body, only Christ gives the orders. If Christians are in conflict, it is because they have not yet understood the Lord's will, or may be misunderstanding the orders from the head, or not getting them from Him at all. They may be still seeking clarity, or be out of touch, mistaking their own desires for the will of Christ. Each part of the Body needs to be in daily touch with the head so directions are not confused.

Fidelity to one Lord is a recurring theme in the New Testament. Speaking to the Gentiles in the home of Cornelius, Peter declared, "God is no respecter of persons. . . . The word which God sent unto the Children of Israel, preaching peace by Jesus Christ" (Acts 10:34, 36). In that parenthetical remark Peter assured the Gentiles that Jesus is their Lord too.

In Romans we also read, "For there is no difference between the Jew and the Greek: for the same Lord over all is rich unto all that call upon Him" (10:12).

And again "But to us there is but one God, the Father, of whom are all things, and we in Him; and one Lord Jesus Christ" (1 Cor. 8:6).

Paul refers next to *one faith* (Eph. 4:5). This may refer to the believer's exercise of saving faith, or it may refer to the content of the Gospel itself, the basic body of Christian truth.

In the first instance, the point is that the believer comes to one Lord by faith. No one comes by any other way. In Paul's day Jew and Gentile asked, "Are there two faith experiences or one?" Paul answered, "Seeing it is one God, which shall justify the circumcision [the Jews] by faith, and uncircumcision [Gentiles] through faith" (Rom. 3:30). All Christians share a common means of salvation.

However, in addition to meaning the believer's response, the word *faith* is also used in Scripture as a body of truth. Jude appeals to believers "to earnestly contend for the faith" (Jude 3). He tells them to build themselves up "in your most holy faith" (v. 20). Paul refers to being "established in the faith" (Col. 2:7).

Here the word refers to the doctrines, in God's revelation to man. In this sense there is only one faith. The Bible is one body of truth. There may be different interpretations of the truth, but there is basically one body of truth. Too often the Body argues about interpretations. We must remember that there is not a Calvinistic New Testament and an Arminian New Testament, not a Baptist New Testament and a Presbyterian New Testament. The Body of Christ holds to one faith.

Each member is responsible to study faithfully and diligently the basic tenets. "Study to show thyself approved unto God, a workman that needeth not to be ashamed, rightly dividing the word of truth," Paul counseled Timothy (2 Tim. 2:15). Not only is a believer to know what the faith teaches, but he is to hold that faith in love. He must forbear when a fellow member of the Body does not see a teaching in the same light. The Body needs prayerful interaction, so that each member may be a corrective to the other. Our goal in the Body should be to express "one faith" simply, clearly, and accurately.

One Baptism for All

Next in the emphases on "ones" is *one baptism* (Eph. 4:5). Bible scholars differ on whether this is the baptism of the Holy Spirit, or the ordinance of water baptism. Since the concept of Spirit baptism is included in one Body, and one Spirit (v. 4), I believe this "baptism" refers to the ordinance.

There's a progression. The Body comprises those who have placed their faith in one Lord, and what follows this expression of faith, according to New Testament practice is the ordinance of baptism. The rite of baptism itself does not save the person, but it is a sign that he has committed himself to Christ.

Baptism is a matter of obedience to the Lord. Jesus included baptism (Matt. 28:19) in the commission to the disciples. The early Christians followed this command. Wherever there was a confession of faith in Christ, there was a public baptism. Believers gave public testimony to their faith that way.

There was no hesitancy about it. The normal pattern was repentance, confession of faith, baptism, acceptance into the local church.

Paul's point of "one baptism" obviously was meant to stress

the oneness of Jew and Gentile. No matter what their origins, when they came to Christ there was one baptism, not different baptisms according to background. The Jews, of course, had practiced distinctive ceremonial washings, and they baptized proselytes. But in the new economy of the Gospel there was to be only one baptism.

Therefore, it is just as essential to obey Christ in baptism as in anything else. It is not an option. It signifies the believer's own identification with the death, burial, and resurrection of Jesus. Water baptism symbolizes the end of the old life and the beginning of the new life. It is a sign to the world of what has transpired in the believer. Baptism follows saving faith, demonstrating by obedience the inner work of the Holy Spirit.

One God and Father of all

The work of the Trinity is revealed in this passage: the Holy Spirit (Eph. 4:4), God the Son (4:5), and God the Father (4:6). Here we have the climax, showing the total unity that is the reason for the believer's worthy walk: *One God.* He is "above all, and through all, and in you all" (4:6). He upholds everything. He sustains and guides the world. What a source of assurance this is to the believer—God is in control!

He expresses His loving and wise control in the believer. The God of the universe is the God of the individual. He is "in you all," that is, in everyone who has trusted in Christ, every member of the Body. The Bible says not even a sparrow falls without His notice. He cares about the seemingly insignificant.

"Know ye not that ye are the temple of God?" (1 Cor. 3:16) We are God-created, God-loved, God-controlled, God-sustained, and God-filled. Believers enjoy the peace and the power that result from having the very life of God in them.

This is the God of the seven-fold unity. God has done everything according to oneness. He wants the Body to display that oneness, even as it is displayed in the Trinity. Everything God planned is one; therefore, it is reasonable that His one Body should act accordingly. Unity is the essence of both the believer's high position and his lowly walk.

7
PERFECTING
THE BODY

(Ephesians 4:11-16)

In the Sermon on the Mount, Jesus made a shocking statement: "Be ye therefore perfect, even as your Father which is in heaven is perfect" (Matt. 5:48). Let's face it: that sets a towering standard.

God's call is for His redeemed people to become *perfect.* The perfection of the Body has been in the redemptive plan of God from eternity past. Throughout history God works to carry out this plan.

When we speak of perfecting the Body, however, we must keep in mind that perfection is used three ways in Scripture. First, there is "positional perfection." When a person receives Jesus Christ, he becomes perfect positionally. "We speak wisdom among them that are perfect" (1 Cor. 2:6). Paul wrote the Colossian believers, "Ye are complete in Him [Christ]" (2:10). The Epistle to the Hebrews holds the same truth: "For the Law made nothing perfect, but the bringing in of a better hope did" (7:19). That "better hope" was Christ. Also, "For by one offering He hath perfected forever them that are sanctified" (Heb. 10:14; 1 Cor. 6:9-11).

Christ makes believers perfect. At the point of his salvation, the believer receives a positional perfection. In receiving Christ's righteousness as his own, his sin is removed and his position in Christ is perfect before God. Therefore, when he dies he may immediately enter God's presence.

The second kind is "ultimate perfection." We read in Hebrews (12:23) about "the spirits of just men made perfect." John writes, "But we know that, when He shall appear we shall be like Him [Christ]; for we shall see Him as He is" (1 John 3:2). When the believer goes to be with God, he attains ultimate perfection. Paul had this in mind when he confessed, "Not as though I had already attained, either were already perfect" (Phil. 3:12). He anticipated attaining "the resurrection of the dead" so that he might achieve ultimate perfection.

Between positional and ultimate perfection is "experiential perfection." Positionally and ultimately believers are perfect, but in experience they are far less. Christ's death and resurrection provided for the Christian's positional and ultimate perfection; His life in the believer provides for experiential perfection.

The whole point of the Christian life is to move toward experiential perfection. Believers are to grow, to mature, to attain practical Christian completeness. Note the phrase, "For the perfecting of the saints" (Eph. 4:12). That refers to experiential perfection of the Body, not to either positional or ultimate perfection. The idea of experiential perfection is also seen in the phrases, "unto a perfect man" (4:13); "be no more children" (4:14); and "grow up into Him" (4:15). The Christian is to attain "the measure of the stature of the fullness of Christ" (4:13). The believer cannot attain sinlessness, but it is possible for him to sin less. He can become a well-rounded, grown-up believer. That is the concern of every member of the Body: to be robust, vigorous, strong, vibrant. Babes in Christ are to grow up, to attain experiential perfection.

The Greek word translated "perfecting" is from *katartismos,* which means "to equip fully." It means something totally complete in itself, full-grown, filled to capacity. No Christian should settle for being less than fully equipped, mature, complete, grown-up, vigorous. Here's the challenge: "Having therefore these promises, dearly beloved, let us cleanse ourselves from all filthiness of the flesh and spirit, perfecting holiness in the fear of God" (2 Cor. 7:1). The whole Body of Christ must be brought to full maturity.

The implication is that the believer is "made perfect" by the Holy Spirit (Gal. 3:3). The Spirit uses trials and suffering to bring this about (James 1:2-4; 1 Peter 5:10). He also uses the Word of God (1 Peter 2:2; 1 Tim. 3:16-17). The Spirit's work is seen in the benediction, "Now the God of peace, that brought again from the dead our Lord Jesus, that great Shepherd of the sheep, through the blood of the everlasting covenant, make you perfect in every good work to do His will" (Heb. 13:20-21).

The most heartbreaking thing in my ministry is not that some people don't respond to the Gospel. It isn't that more people don't go to the mission field, but that some members of the Body remain spiritual babies all their lives.

God's plan to bring believers to maturity includes, with the work of the Holy Spirit, human instruments, also. "And He gave some, apostles; and some, prophets; and some, evangelists; and some, pastors and teachers" (Eph. 4:11).

Why did God give these? "For the perfecting of the saints." "Saints" are believers, all members of the Body. God gave the early Church apostles and prophets to perfect the saints. He gave evangelists and teaching-pastors to perfect the saints.

Apostles, prophets, evangelists, pastor-teachers—all are gifted men given to the Body of Christ so that Christians might be brought to perfection. We will examine the character of each office in the next chapter of this book. Here we simply want to note God's basic plan. These men are the agents of change in the life of the Church; they are channels for the flow of dynamic energy for spiritual growth; they are catalysts for experiential perfection. The result of their ministry is the Body built up in love (Eph. 4:16).

We note three features of experiential perfection: (1) the progress to perfection; (2) its purposes; (3) its power (4:11-16).

Progress to Perfection

Paul outlines specific steps in the Body's maturing process. First, gifted men equip the saints (4:11-12). The Lord Jesus Christ won gifted men at the cross and gave them to the Church so that His children might be perfectly equipped and mature in their faith. These gifted ones have specific ministries to this end. Spiritual gifts for believers *en masse* are not in view here, but for those whom God has appointed as leaders among the total Body. Their ministries are listed chronologically according to God's plan for the development of the Church.

The apostles were a small group, originally appointed by Jesus Himself. They stood in unique relation to the incarnate Lord. They were His constant companions, witnesses to what He said and did, "sent ones" to preach, heal, and cast out demons. After the defection of Judas, Matthias was chosen to fill the ranks. To the Twelve Jesus gave the Great Commission. They were to become the authoritative source of the truth about Christ, as John explained: "That which was from the beginning, which we have heard, which we have seen with our eyes, which we have looked upon, and our hands have handled . . . declare we unto you" (1 John 1:1, 3).

Besides the Twelve, one other man belonged to the Christ-appointed apostles. Because Jesus revealed Himself directly and spoke to him, Paul rightfully claimed apostleship (Eph. 1:1; Col. 1:1; Gal. 1:1). His unique call and commission formed the basis of his authority in the churches (Acts 9).

Others who would fall into a secondary group of apostles are Barnabas, Silas, Timothy, and lesser-known men such as Andronicus and Junia (Rom. 16:7). They were apostles of the Church, but not directly commissioned by the risen Lord.

The Foundation of Doctrine

Apostles had a specific purpose in God's plan. The Church was "built upon the foundation of the apostles and prophets" (Eph. 2:20). Among other things, the mystery of the Church was revealed through the "holy apostles and prophets by the

Spirit" (Eph. 3:5). The apostles preached the truth that became the foundation of Christian doctrine. The early Church subsisted on "the apostles' doctrine" (Acts 2:42). The gifted men affirmed God's truth authoritatively, based on the Old Testament Scriptures and what they had witnessed of Christ's teachings, death, and resurrection.

God confirmed apostolic authority by giving the ability to perform miracles. God authenticated their teaching "with signs and wonders, and with divers miracles" (Heb. 2:4), and "with the signs of an apostle" (2 Cor. 12:12).

In the history of the early Church, as recorded in Acts, the last time the apostles met as a body was at the Council of Jerusalem. After that, except for John and Paul and his fellow-laborers, they disappear from the historical records. As the Gospel spread and churches were founded, leadership fell to faithful men who followed the apostolic teaching. The apostles laid the foundation and brought the Church to birth, so to speak. They planted churches and taught new believers in the faith. But gradually local elders supplanted them. The tiny assemblies began to operate for themselves. As the building grew, the foundation was no longer in sight. So, the apostles as such were a temporary group of men, not a permanent fixture in the Church (see Eph. 2:20). No one today may rightfully claim to be a part of this unique group.

Paul does not refer in Ephesians to Old Testament prophets but to New Testament ones, another temporary group of gifted men given to the infant Church. Linked with the apostles (Eph. 2:20; 3:5), these men were needed as God's spokesmen. The New Testament did not exist. These prophets spoke directly from God, as did the Old Testament prophets.

This could lead to a problem, if a prophet began to give forth as authoritative something that was his own idea. For this reason Paul ordered that "the spirits of the prophets are subject to the prophets" (1 Cor. 14:32). These men were to check on each other during the course of their ministries (14:29).

Such prophetic ministry ceased with the writing of the New Testament. Today God doesn't speak to the Church by direct revelation to individuals. His "direct revelation" is in the words of Scripture, inspired by the Holy Spirit, inerrant and authoritative for the believer. The foundational ministry of apostles and prophets is past and no longer needed. God's revelation in the Bible is complete, emphatically warning against adding to it or subtracting from it (Rev. 22:18-19). Believers need not seek direct prophetic revelation today; they need to know the Bible.

The New Testament picture of an evangelist is of a man who goes from place to place where the Gospel has not been preached. He preaches Christ and leads people to faith in Him. He teaches the resulting believers basic doctrine, stays until they mature, then appoints elders, and moves on to the next place. He is basically a planter of churches. The New Testament evangelist is not a person who comes to town for a week of meetings and then leaves. His work isn't finished until he has founded a church. Timothy and Philip are examples.

Protecting the Flock

The office of pastor-teacher is one, not two. The idea is a teaching shepherd. He stays in one place, teaching the Gospel and sound doctrine, while at the same time pastoring the sheep. He takes over when the evangelist leaves. His task is to feed and lead the Church.

The teaching shepherd's main task is to protect the flock. That's what shepherding is—protecting from both dangerous places and enemies. The pastor-teacher does this by building safeguards, teaching the truth, and helping those who may be stumbling into sin. He not only preserves them, but strengthens and encourages them. Jesus, of course, is the chief Shepherd. He loves His Flock. He builds His Church. He does so by providing the Body with gifted men—evangelists and pastor-teachers.

The Body needs to recognize God's plan. In some churches, leadership is, in effect, removed from gifted men in the name of spontaneity and freedom of the Spirit. It is a serious error to think, "We'll just get together and see how the Spirit leads."

In God's plan for the Body, the Holy Spirit does not have responsibility for church order or planning services. In fact, at Corinth in the early Church, a problem developed because of an apparent failure on the part of the ruling gifted men. There may have been some, but no elders are mentioned at Corinth. The believers tried to do their own thing, and this reaped chaos and confusion. So Paul rebuked them (1 Cor. 14:23-24) and reminded them that God is not the author of confusion. Order is the responsibility of gifted men whom God gives to the Church. Whenever local church order is set loose, without careful guidance of Spirit-led, gifted men, the chances are great that some people will participate who are not Spirit-led. What occurs may be more sociological and psychological than biblical. The results are uncertain, confusing, and perhaps even demonic.

We see that church planters and teaching shepherds have replaced apostles and prophets in the Body. But the task is the same as that of the original apostles and prophets: to bring believers to perfection. Their work does not cease anywhere short of maturity in the lives of their flock. Their task is not to fill the building, but to equip the saints.

This passion for maturity in the Body stands out in the New Testament writers. Note, for example, Paul's statement to the Colossians. "Whom we preach [Christ], warning every man, and teaching every man in all wisdom; that we may present every man perfect in Christ Jesus" (1:28). Paul would settle for nothing less than maturity.

Then there was Epaphras, "a servant of Christ . . . always laboring fervently for you in prayers, that ye may stand *perfect* and *complete* in all the will of God" (Col. 4:12, italics added). Epaphras is not famous like Paul, but he prayed passionately that every member of the Body would reach maturity. This is always to be the passion of gifted men. The call to the ministry is not a call to a profession; but to a passion. God gives gifted men to the Church, not to entertain it, program it, or organize it, but to bring believers to maturity. Nothing less satisfies the man of God (James 1:4; Heb. 13:20-21).

The question is, "How does the man of God 'perfect the saints'?" How is this done in the local church today? The answer is threefold: "Preach the word" (2 Tim. 4:2), "Be instant [diligent] in season, out of season; and reprove, rebuke, exhort with all long-suffering and doctrine." Preach the word! Hosea said, "My people are destroyed for lack of knowledge" (Hosea 4:6). The Word of God must be taught to renew the mind before life can become perfect (Rom. 12:2; Eph. 4:23). Paul tells us that teaching perfects, and thus he is totally committed to it (Col. 1:28).

Paul expressed this command to Timothy in different ways. "All Scripture is given by inspiration of God, and is profitable for doctrine, for reproof, for correction, for instruction in righteousness: That the man of God may be perfect, thoroughly furnished unto all good works" (2 Tim. 3:16-17).

"If thou put the brethren in remembrance of these things, thou shalt be a good minister of Jesus Christ, nourished up in the words of faith and of good doctrine" (1 Tim. 4:6).

Timothy's job was to transmit the things he learned to faithful men who in turn could teach others (2 Tim. 2:2).

This pattern works in the ministry today. It is still God's plan: teach men who will teach others, who will in turn teach others, and so on. Teach what? The Word of God. Experiential perfection of the members of the Body develops through the Word of God.

Scripture Perfects!

Of course, the pastor-teacher himself must be a "workman" in the Word. He cannot teach it unless he studies it. This is part of his primary responsibility: study and teach the Word. The Word of God taught by men of God brings growth in the people of God.

That basic directive, "perfecting the saints," is the heart of the pastor's ministry. Anything less is a perversion. Spending time on other things is to miss God's basic calling. The pastor's heart should throb with the plea of Paul: "Night and day praying exceedingly that we might see your face, and might perfect that which is lacking in your faith" (1 Thes. 3:10).

One of the tenderest scenes recorded in the Bible took place the day Paul left Ephesus, after three years of "perfecting the saints" there. Every evangelist and teaching pastor should prayerfully study it. In it Paul characterizes his ministry in simple terms: "I . . . have *taught* you publicly, and from house to house. . . . I have not shunned to declare unto you *all the counsel* of God" (Acts 20:20, 27, italics added).

Paul had systematically taught Bible doctrine. Now he was leaving the same responsibility to the elders, the teaching pastors who would remain. He sets forth the reason for this commission: the value of the Church to God, the inevitability of false teachers moving in with perverse dogma, and the inability of anything else to build up the saints to maturity.

The final words of the farewell speak in the most beautiful way of how believers will respond if the man of God properly teaches them: "And when he had thus spoken, he kneeled down, and prayed with them all. And they all wept sore, and fell on Paul's neck, and kissed him, sorrowing most of all for the words which he spake."

It was his "words"—the instruction in doctrine—that endeared him most to them. The people of God need the Word of God, and when it is given and bears fruit in their lives, their gratitude is a sweet reward.

Teaching Believers

The second stage in the progress to perfection is what believers themselves do. "For the perfecting of the saints for the work of the ministry" (Eph. 4:12). Why do gifted men equip the saints? So that they might do the work of the ministry. The gifted men are to teach the Word to equip the saints to do the work. Teaching is the pastor's job.

Too often, however, this biblical pattern is thwarted by church members who expect pastors to do everything. No wonder some pastors suffer so much physical and emotional fatigue. Some have been driven to breakdowns. They can't find the time to study the Word of God because their church members expect them not only to equip the saints, but to do the work of the ministry also. That is not God's plan for the Body.

His plan is well illustrated by an incident in the early Church. A dispute arose because certain widows were being neglected in the daily dispensing of food. The apostles resolved the matter with a significant decision. They told the Church to appoint seven Spirit-filled men to look after the distribution of food, because "we will give ourselves continually to prayer, and to the ministry of the Word" (Acts 6:4).

The apostles were not being proud or lazy. They were not above menial work. They were not above visiting people. But they were establishing a priority for their own ministry. They saw that their distinct contribution to the Body was praying and teaching the Word to equip the saints for the ministry. They rigidly adhered to the reason why God gave gifted men to the Church.

The apostles also recognized that the Body needs all members. There was a "work of the ministry" for each to perform. In fact, these parallel ministries of the gifted men and the members of the Body show that the modern functional split between clergy and laymen is a false one. It destroys the beauty of the Body. The gifted men given to the Church are no better than the individual members; in God's plan He simply chose some to have the privilege of preaching and teaching. Having that role in the plan of God does not elevate them qualitatively, just as it doesn't require them to be looking after a host of details unrelated to their primary callings. The dynamic of the early Church came from a proper understanding of roles in the Body: gifted men building up the saints, who in turn exercise spiritual ministries throughout the Body. None greater than the other, but each fulfilling his calling.

Here we need to define "the work of the ministry for the edifying of the Body" (Eph. 4:12) which the believers are called on to perform. There are many church activities that cannot legitimately be called spiritual ministries, even though they are useful to the church program. This is not to minimize any activity—even putting up posters, for that matter—but it is to emphasize that the publicity chairman should also have a personal, spiritual ministry in the building of the Body.

Exercising Gifts

God has given each member certain spiritual gifts (to be discussed in chapter 8) for the work of the ministry. These spiritual gifts can be exercised in many ways: visiting the sick and shut-ins, counseling new Christians, praying and studying the Bible with others, taking food, clothes, and money to people in special need, showing personal love and care for the lonely and discouraged, reaching out to neighbors and friends with the Gospel.

The local church essentially is a training place to equip Christians to carry out their own ministries. Unfortunately, for many Christians the church is a place to go to watch professionals perform and to pay the professionals to carry out the church program. In many quarters Christianity has deteriorated into professional "pulpitism," financed by lay spectators. The church hires a staff of ministers to do all the Christian service.

This scheme is not only a violation of God's plan, but an absolute detriment to the growth of the Church and the vitality of the members of the Body. Every member needs to find a significant place of service. To limit the work of the ministry to a small, select class of full-time clergymen hinders the spiritual growth of God's people, stunts the discipleship process in the Body, and the evangelistic outreach of the church into the community.

From the members who give themselves to the work of the ministry God Himself will choose certain ones to be His gifts to the Church as a whole. This is a never-ending cycle. Every congregation ought to be producing faithful workers, some of whom in turn will be called by God to become full-time evangelists and pastor-teachers. This is exactly what happened in Philip's life. His ministry began as a Spirit-filled deacon (Acts 6:5), and then God called him to a wide evangelistic ministry (Acts 8:5-40). Those called by God will then be used by Him to train others, and from those God will in turn call more gifted ones. This is basic to His plan for the perfection of the Body.

I am more and more committed to the proposition that each local church ought to be developing its own spiritual leadership. Instead of bringing in outside men to fill these positions, the church ought to develop its own people to spiritual maturity. If a church is not producing competent leaders to serve Christ in a full-time capacity, something is wrong.

At Grace Community Church our gifted evangelists and pastor-teachers have come from within the ranks of the congregation. God has brought them to maturity by His Spirit, through His Word. These people were "faithful in a little," so to speak, and God gave them a larger responsibility. The result for our church has been a unique quality of unity, fellowship, and commitment to each other—leaders and flock alike— which is more difficult to achieve if the ministering staff is assembled from outside the congregation. The first level of my ministry has been to "disciple" these people. Our staff has grown from the soil of much time that we have spent with each one in personal discipling, teaching, and prayer. Others have grown and been sent out to mission fields and other churches.

In fact, though we pray and work for souls to be saved, we have never deliberately sought more people to swell our numbers. We have no right to ask God for more people until we see progress in those He has already given us to equip. Thank God, there has been progress. We see the saints feeding and loving each other, counseling each other, caring for each other, nourishing each other, and even developing, organizing, and operating various ministries within the church.

I remember seeing, at a circus, a man spinning plates on eight sticks. He would get all eight going and have to run back to keep the first one moving, and so on up the line. This seems to me an apt illustration of the role of the pastor, who has figured out the plates he wants to spin and looks through the congregation to find the right sticks. He gets all going and discovers that the sticks don't keep the plates moving, so he is stuck with running up and down from plate to plate, filling in for the inoperative sticks. How much better it is to concentrate all on "perfecting the saints" so that as they grow they become motivated to begin certain ministries that are on their hearts and which interest them. Perfected, mature saints will develop ministries in the energy and excitement of their maturity.

As a result the Body of Christ is edified (Eph. 4:12). When each member performs his ministry, the whole Body comes to maturity.

When the Body is built up, more people are won to Christ. A strong, unified, loving, serving Body has a dynamic testimony to the world. For the Body to be built up, every part must be involved—gifted men perfecting the saints, and the saints doing the work of the ministry. That is the progress of perfection.

What are the results of experiential perfection? Paul specifies five of them (Eph. 4:13-15):

"Unity of the faith" is one (4:13). If gifted men equip the saints, and the saints do the work of the ministry, the Body grows and believers are united. The Body that is mature and working and serving will be united. If sometimes there is breakdown, it is because either the pastor doesn't teach the Word to equip the believers, or the believers do not accept their responsibility of ministry.

Because the whole Body is affected, it disturbs me to see pastors and evangelists who are not teaching the Word. They have active programs, but their schedules are so busy that they do not study the Word and teach it in every service.

"They continued steadfastly in the apostles' doctrine and

fellowship, and in breaking of bread, and in prayers" (Acts 2:42). This is our biblical pattern. This preserves unity in the Body. "The multitude of them that believed were of one heart and of one soul; neither said any of them that aught [any] of the things which he possessed was his own; but they had all things common" (4:32).

These believers also had great boldness and power in their witness to Christ. They won people to Him every day (2:47).

Because they gave themselves to the study of the Word and ministered to each other, their love and unity had a profound impact on the world. If the Body is to be one, it cannot break down at any point.

Another result when the believer follows God's purpose for perfection is that he comes to *"the knowledge of the Son of God"* (4:13). This follows his growth in understanding the Word of God, his growth in maturity, his growth in personal ministry, and his growth in oneness. Some Christians' knowledge of Christ is limited to His saving work on their behalf. In God's purpose the believer is to grow in more intimate fellowship with Christ. The body that is learning and serving will be deeply involved with Jesus Christ. The maturing Christian experiences an increasingly richer personal fellowship with the Son of God.

Becoming more like Jesus Christ is another part of experiential perfection. This results from deeper, more intimate fellowship with Him. Paul describes the believer's goal: "unto a perfect man" (4:13). The word implies a fully developed, robust, mature person. God is not satisfied when we accept anything less for our standard. The perfect man, of course, is Christ; to measure how mature you are, how perfect, you must compare yourself with Him. No one has arrived spiritually until he attains Christ's stature. Once in a while a person thinks he has made a great spiritual stride, but lest he think there's no further to go, Paul keeps the standard before him: "the fullness of Christ."

God's plan for moving toward that fullness is plain: teach the Word, equip the saints for the work of ministry, unity in the

Body, a deeper knowledge of Christ. Each believer finds himself involved somewhere in this process of spiritual growth and development. He keeps moving toward the goal: to be like Jesus. Jesus shows the Christian God's perfection and then says, "Be like Me."

It's easy, of course, to stop at some lower level, but the progressively perfected believer will settle for nothing less than the fullness of Christ. He will constantly strive to be like Jesus in everything he does, not just so he can say that he has achieved something, but because he wants to show his love and reverence for Christ. I want to be like Jesus because I love Him.

One day I asked my son, Mark, what he wanted to be when he grew up.

"I'm going to be a dad, just like you," he said.

"Well, why do you want to be a dad just like me?" I asked him.

"Because I love you," he said.

He wanted to be like me because he loves and respects me. Since I am the object of his love as his father, he wants to emulate me.

Becoming like Jesus

If Christians really love Jesus, they will want to be like Him. If they don't care enough to try to be like Him, perhaps their professions of love for Him are a sham.

Solid in doctrine is the fourth result of experiential perfection. "That we henceforth be no more children, tossed to and fro, and carried about with every wind of doctrine, by the sleight of men, and cunning craftiness, whereby they lie in wait to deceive." (Eph. 4:14).

Children are gullible and undiscerning. They don't know what's good or bad. Give them a choice of diet, and they'll get sick. Children will believe anyone. God's purpose in perfecting His children is that in the spiritual realm they will not act like gullible, undiscerning children when it comes to doctrine. They are not to be susceptible to every new religious fad. They are to be strong, firm, confident of what they believe—not tossed about by the shifting winds of ungodly philosophies.

Some Christians, because they are spiritual babies, fall victim to false teaching. But if a believer follows God's plan for perfection, is well taught, and gives himself to spiritual ministry, he is not going to be swayed by error. Rather than being thrown off by it, he will be able to expose it. God's will is for every believer to grow up out of spiritual childhood and so not be susceptible when "crafty" deceivers come around.

In 1 John 2:13-14, John speaks of levels of spiritual growth. The second level, "young men," are those who conquer Satan. Since Satan's major effort is in false doctrine (see 2 Cor. 11:14), it indicates that only those who have grown from babies to young men spiritually can deal with the problem.

Evangelism—"Speaking the truth in love" (Eph. 4:15)—is the last result of perfecting the Body. The climax is the proclamation of God's truth, in love, by every believer, both to other believers and to the unbeliever. This is the end result for the Christian who really knows Christ, who wants to be like Him, who is strong in faith and doctrine. Proclaiming the truth is the believer's work of the ministry, something he himself can do in his community and at work.

God's plan of perfection for the Body then is progressive. He gives gifted men to the Church to equip the saints. The saints thus equipped do the work of the ministry. The Body grows and is built up. The Body comes together in unity. Individual members have a deep, abiding fellowship with Christ. They grow in Christlikeness; they know sound doctrine, combat false teaching, and go into the community with a dynamic, loving presentation of the Gospel.

In discussing the perfection of the believer in the Body, it is easy to get the impression that everything depends on us. True, Scripture clearly outlines human responsibility—gifted men are to teach, the saints are to respond and grow. If that were the end of the matter it would be just another humanistic scheme. But perfection is not achieved by human strength.

Notice that the connecting word between Ephesians 4:15 and 16 is "Christ: From whom the whole Body fitly joined together and compacted by that which every joint supplieth, according to the effectual working in the measure of every part, maketh increase of the Body unto the edifying of itself in love."

The Body's growth is from Jesus Christ. Christ is the source of the power to make the progress and purposes of perfection actually happen. "Christ, from whom the whole thing happens." Without this statement, perfection appears to rest solely with the individual. But the power is really Jesus Christ's, working in and through the believer. And the power of Christ bringing the perfection of the Body will be unleashed when the Word of God is faithfully proclaimed and when the saints do the work of the ministry.

8
THE GIFTS OF THE BODY

(Romans 12:3-8; 1 Corinthians 12:1-11)

God wants to reach the whole world with His truth, therefore, the Holy Spirit has specially empowered and enabled members of the Body to carry out some very important functions. In the Old Testament, Israel was God's vehicle to reach the world. In the New Testament era Jesus and His disciples were God's vehicles. Today God uses the Church to communicate to the world His nature and His truth.

The Church's witness is not only verbal; it is not only a communication of the Gospel in specifics; it is the witness of love and unity. When believers are one in love, the world will find their witness impressive. A unity, built on humility and love, becomes the Church's greatest testimony. Though believers have been made one in terms of the Holy Spirit's ministry of placing them into the Body of Christ, and though they are one in the Holy Spirit, they are not one in spirit. The world does not see them as one in practice. They do not have a singular testimony of humility and love.

Satan wants them to be divided. So, while the prayer of Christ was that Christians be one, and while the activity of the Holy Spirit is to make them one, all of the energy of Satan is to fracture Christian unity. Whenever a divisive issue arises within the Body of Christ, we can be sure one side is the agent of Satan. Christ wants to unify; Satan wants to divide. There are so many disobedient Christians that Satan has been tremendously successful.

There is no scriptural justification for all the present divisions of the Church. There were no denominations in the New Testament. In fact, church divisions are explicitly contrary to the teaching of the Word of God. Christ's intent in forming the Body was that believers be one, not divided into little parts.

The Body was formed in unity, not in discord. In the Book of Acts we read that the Church began in a prayer meeting in the Upper Room of a house in Jerusalem. The disciples of Jesus gathered there to pray. Out of their faith, obedience, and waiting in prayer, God brought into being the Church. Men and women filled with the Holy Spirit, and possessing gifts of the Holy Spirit, went out of the room into the streets to preach Christ crucified and risen. They were humble people. There were no great ones. They had no organizational structure; but they "turned the world upside down."

That was the birth of the Church—the Body of Christ. It was accomplished in the energy of the Holy Spirit. From that moment, every member has been added to the church the same way—by the Spirit placing him into the Body of Christ (1 Cor. 12:13). Christians are as organically one today as they were in Acts 2.

The early Church was exciting. Believers were all filled with the Spirit. They were all exercising their spiritual gifts. They were preaching the Gospel. They had a unity of humble love that was manifest everywhere. The world was shaken. People couldn't believe what was happening in Jerusalem. People were added daily to the Church.

In order for the Church today to be an effective witness it must be as spiritually healthy as the early Church. Not just organized, but Spirit-filled. Not just super-committed, but exercising spiritual gifts. Not just giving out publicity, but preaching the Gospel. The standards have not changed. Christians must be mature, loving, and humble. They must be Spirit-filled and exercising gifts, just as those in the early Church did.

God's Plan for the Church

Christ wants the Church to be powerful; He wants the Church to be mature; He wants the Church to be functioning, to be growing, to be witnessing, and manifesting His love. In order to accomplish this, God designed a plan for the Church. This is God's plan. Besides the gifted man given to the church (Eph. 4:11-12) to make the church really grow and have a unified witness, God desires every member to have a certain function, or functions, within the body. Every member must have a ministry that lends itself to the health of that body. The human body is an illustration of this. It has all kinds of organs that interact. If just one of these organs doesn't function, the whole body feels it. The same thing is true of the Body of Christ; every member has a function that affects the health of the whole Body. Every believer has a necessary ministry as a vital organ of the Body. If the Body is to be healthy and mature, and thus have a single dynamic testimony to the world, every believer must actively and intensely involve himself in the function God has given him. His services and ministry make the Body healthy because he carries strength to the other vital parts. His failure to serve cripples the Body.

The total Body is to be like Jesus Christ (Eph. 4:13). Through the Church Christ wants to manifest His own character; He wants to manifest His person through believers, not only as individuals but as a Body. To accomplish this, God gives every member a certain spiritual gift to minister to the rest of the Body.

This identification of the gifts with Christ can be seen in the fact that all the spiritual gifts are, in their fullest sense, complete and perfectly operative in Christ: preaching, teaching—no matter what the gift, Christ used it to the fullest extent. The reason God gives each believer differing gifts is that He wants the Body to manifest a composite Christlikeness. The gifts are not random; they are Christ's characteristics reproduced by the Spirit in the Body. This means that the only way an individual Christian will ever be a man of full stature in Christ is when all gifts are ministered to him. A

Christian can never be completely like Jesus Christ until he has been built up in all the areas represented by spiritual gifts.

This is why each believer must minister his gift to another believer. As one ministers to another, he builds him up in that area. If I minister the gift of preaching, my people should learn from my ministering how to communicate more effectively. If a believer in my church has the gift of showing mercy, and he ministers that gift to me, I not only receive the direct blessing and purpose of that gift, but I learn a little more about how to show mercy. I may not have that gift, but in a lesser degree, I'm built up in that area. As each member ministers to the other, all are built up as individuals to be like Christ and to show forth His attributes. Collectively, they manifest the total person of Christ. This is not meant to imply that all believers should minister all categories of gifts, nor that each Christian becomes a body by himself. But each is to reflect Christ.

From 1 Corinthians 12 we learn the importance of spiritual gifts, their source, their power, and their extent. First, the importance of spiritual gifts is seen in Paul's statement, "Now concerning spiritual gifts, brethren, I would not have you ignorant" (1 Cor. 12:1). Unfortunately, some believers are ignorant. The Corinthian believers were grossly ignorant. Some people abuse the spiritual gifts, some neglect them. Some Christians emphasize only the sign gifts, the miraculous gifts, and ignore the edifying ones. It is essential for the ministry of the Church that Christians understand spiritual gifts. No congregation will be what the Holy Spirit gifted it and empowered it to be, until it understands and exercises spiritual gifts.

The Source of Spiritual Gifts

The Holy Spirit is the source of the spiritual gifts. God gives these gifts through the Spirit and distributes them to the Body members. "But all these [Paul has just referred to the spiritual gifts] worketh that one and the selfsame Spirit, dividing to every man severally as He will" (1 Cor. 12:11). The day the Christian was born into the family of God, the day that he received Jesus Christ as his personal Saviour, the Spirit of God distributed to him a spiritual gift.

A spiritual gift is a channel through which the Holy Spirit ministers to the Body. It is not the end in itself. Every believer has a spiritual gift, regardless of his personal spiritual development. Possession of a spiritual gift does not mean a Christian is "spiritual." The question is whether the channel is clear or plugged up. Many people think that when they have attained some spiritual gifts they are instantly made spiritual. One conceivably might have all of the gifts recorded in Scripture and still be unspiritual. This was true of the assembly at Corinth (1 Cor. 1:7; 3:1-4).

Some people think they should seek certain gifts. They are told to "tarry" for certain gifts. Some even follow gimmicks and techniques to get them. They attempt to generate artificial, emotional, and even satanic activity, and then call such activity the gifts of the Spirit. The Holy Spirit is the source of spiritual *gifts,* not self-induced hysteria, not satanic counterfeits. The Holy Spirit gives the gifts by divine will and divine choice. He knows what gifts are needed, where they are needed, when they are needed, and who is to receive them.

It is also true that one can have a gift from the Holy Spirit and be doing nothing about it. Paul told Timothy, "Neglect not the gift that is in thee" (1 Tim. 4:14).

Timothy had become sidetracked by certain people who were pressuring him. He was getting upset. He had his gift but he neglected it. Evidently Timothy still wasn't doing too well later, prompting Paul to write, "Wherefore I put thee in remembrance that thou stir up the gift of God" (2 Tim. 1:6).

A spiritual gift is not the same as a natural ability. You can't say, "My gift is making pie." That's a wonderful ability, but that is not a gift of the Spirit. Or some may say, "My gift is to work with my hands," or "My gift is to sing." Those are not spiritual gifts; those are natural abilities. The spiritual gifts are sovereignly bestowed manifestations of the Spirit's power.

The Apostle Paul illustrates the difference between a spiritual gift and a natural ability. He obviously had natural ability to express himself publicly; but it is clear that he never regarded his ability to speak as a gift of the Spirit. He also was a man of tremendous learning. He could have used his knowledge of philosophy and literature to compose eloquent, convincing orations. He could have delivered them with magnificent ability. But he said this: "And I, brethren, when I came to you, came not with excellency of speech or of wisdom, declaring unto you the testimony of God. For I determined not to know any thing among you, except Jesus Christ, and Him crucified" (1 Cor. 2:1-2).

The Holy Spirit expresses Himself through men. He uses a man's knowledge and ability, but in a supernatural way apart from man's own ability.

Many people have the gift of gab, and they aren't preachers. If a man has a natural aptitude along that line, perhaps the Holy Spirit will elect to use it; perhaps He won't.

On the other hand, I recall a friend in seminary who had a severe stuttering problem. My first reaction when I heard him in preaching class was, "There is no way that he belongs in the ministry as a preacher." Today he is a fine Bible teacher, an able expositor of the Word of God, and a lucid speaker, even though he still struggles with words. He does not have a natural gift of eloquence, but he has the gift of preaching and teaching.

So God may elect to use a Christian's natural ability, or He may give him a spiritual gift that has no connection with his natural ability. Relying on natural ability for the production of spiritual fruit is a hindrance to what the Spirit wants to do. In 1 Peter 4:10-11 we read:

> As every man hath received the gift, even so minister the same one to another, as good stewards of the manifold grace of God. If any man speak, let him speak as the oracles of God; if any man minister, let him do it as of the ability which God giveth, that God in all things may be glorified through Jesus Christ, to whom be praise and dominion forever and ever.

It is important to note that Peter says "the gift." This

indicates a singular gift and is consistent with Paul's use of "the gift" (1 Tim. 4:14; 2 Tim. 1:6). I believe it indicates that each believer receives one gift—unique to him, but that gift may combine elements from all the categories of giftedness. Each believer is, then, a spiritual "snowflake"! This understanding also allows for the obvious diversity of each believer.

In the Spirit or in the Flesh?

There is a difference between the ability to speak and the Spirit-given gift of preaching. On the other hand, it is possible for a man to have the gift of preaching, yet stand in the pulpit and preach in the flesh. I can verify, by personal experience, that it is a constant battle in my own heart and mind not to speak humanly, but as the oracle of God, to bring my gifts into subjection to the Holy Spirit.

The fact that one has a spiritual gift doesn't necessarily mean he always ministers it in the Holy Spirit. "And the spirits of the prophets are subject to the prophets" (1 Cor. 14:32). This means that even one called to be a preacher (prophet) has to subject his spirit. I am not spiritual because I preach. "Let the prophets speak two or three, and let the others judge" (1 Cor. 14:29). The prophets are fallible, so they must check each other to verify what they say. Spiritual gifts are no guarantee that a believer is always right.

In summary, we have seen that a Christian possessing a spiritual gift is not necessarily spiritual and that gifts given by the Holy Spirit are not necessarily in accordance with natural ability. A believer can minister his gift in the energy of either the Spirit or of the flesh.

A person can know nothing about Christianity and spiritual gifts if the Holy Spirit does not teach him. Even something as basic as the lordship of Christ cannot be known unless the Holy Spirit reveals it. When Peter said to Jesus, "Thou art the Christ, the Son of the living God," Jesus replied, "Flesh and blood hath not revealed it unto thee, but My Father which is in heaven" (Matt. 16:16-17).

"Ye know that ye were Gentiles, carried away unto these

dumb idols, even as ye were led" (1 Cor. 12:2). The word "led" refers to leading a prisoner. The unsaved person is seen in a kind of pathetic hopelessness, worshiping false gods who cannot speak because they do not exist. "Wherefore I give you to understand, that no man speaking by the Spirit of God calleth Jesus accursed: and that no man can say that Jesus is the Lord, but by the Holy Ghost" (12:3).

To paraphrase Paul, "I don't want you to be ignorant about spiritual gifts, but you couldn't know about them, because you don't know the basics. You couldn't know about spiritual gifts, until you knew the lordship of Christ, and you couldn't know that apart from the Holy Spirit." The flesh is incapable of knowing anything (1 Cor. 2:10). If the natural man can't understand the lordship of Christ, how can he understand the work of the Holy Spirit through spiritual gifts? Spiritual understanding and spiritual work can only be done by the power of the Spirit. Jesus said, "Ye shall receive power, after that the Holy Ghost is come upon you" (Acts 1:8). The Holy Spirit, then, is the power for understanding and for operating spiritual gifts.

Whatever a Christian does on his own, in his own flesh, in his own fashion, in his own will and design, is a waste and mockery. But whatever he does by the Holy Spirit's power is borne along by divine energy. A Christian doesn't have to build up his strength himself. He must say, "Spirit of God, use me," for divine energy to flow to the Body as he ministers. Every member's gift must be exercised in the energy of the Holy Spirit if it is to be effective. The Corinthian believers had the gifts, but through carnality they had quenched and grieved the Holy Spirit. No power was coming through. The Corinthian part of the Body was sick.

There are three steps to using one's gift in the energy of the Spirit. (1) Prayer. Constantly ask God to cleanse your life, to use you in the Spirit's power. (2) Yield yourself (Rom. 6:16; 12:1-2). (3) Be filled with the Holy Spirit (Eph. 5:18). Allow the Spirit of God to permeate every aspect of your life. Turn every decision, thought, and attitude over to the Spirit's control. Commit all to Him.

Gifts That Build Up

There appear to be two kinds of spiritual gifts: permanent and temporary. Permanent gifts edify or build up the Body. These are the gifts which do not cease. They began in the early Church and still go on today.

The gift of prophecy. The gift of prophecy means preaching, not foretelling the future. It means "to tell forth, to declare." It is important to understand that there is a gift of prophecy and there is a gifted man called a prophet (see chapter 7). The gift of prophecy is not to be confused with the office of prophet. We read, "For to one is given by the Spirit the word of wisdom . . . to another prophecy" (1 Cor. 12:8, 10). This is the gift of prophecy. God has not only given every member of the Body of Christ certain gifts, He has also given the Church certain gifted men. "And God hath set some in the church, first apostles, secondarily prophets, thirdly teachers" (1 Cor. 12:28). They are men, not gifts. The prophet and the gift of prophecy are thus distinct. The New Testament prophets belonged to a special group for a special time in history. They spoke the Word of God directly. They belonged to the first century Church, the apostolic era. There are no prophets today, any more than there are Christ-appointed apostles. The Word of God is complete. No further revelation is being given.

Though the prophets have ceased, the gift of prophecy, or preaching, still goes on to confirm the revelation already given. That's why Paul says, "Follow after charity, and desire spiritual gifts, but rather that ye may prophesy" (1 Cor. 14:1). The word *prophesy* means "preach." Preaching is defined by Paul's use of three words. "But he that prophesieth [preaches] speaketh unto men to edification, and exhortation, and comfort" (14:3). Preaching is building up, encouraging, and comforting. The best way to preach is given by Paul to Timothy in these words: "Til I come, given attendance to reading, to exhortation, to doctrine" (1 Tim. 4:13). Paul advocates expository preaching here as he says, in effect, "Read the text, explain the text, apply the text." The implication is that much preaching only departs from the text.

Comparing the gift of prophecy with tongues, Paul says, "He that speaketh in an unknown tongue edifieth himself, but he that prophesieth edifieth the Church" (1 Cor. 14:4). Preaching was a dominant ministry.

There are some efforts today to play down the centrality of preaching, but preaching is still a gift of the Spirit. No service of the Body is complete without a declaration of God's truth. The preaching of the Cross is still central in the gathering of the Church. The standard of true preaching was whether or not the prophet's words squared with the words of Jesus Christ (1 Cor. 14:37). The gift of preaching today is exercised under the same standard. The standard for preaching is not *Time* magazine, *Newsweek,* or politics. It's not someone's philosophy or a book review. It's the Word of God. Preaching *(kerygma)* always includes biblical doctrine (*didache*). The gift of preaching is a Spirit-given and Spirit-energized ability to proclaim the truths of Jesus Christ. All Christians are witnesses of Christ.

The gift of teaching. The gift of teaching is distinct from the teacher. There is a gift of teaching, and there is a gifted man, a teacher (1 Cor. 12:28). The office of teaching did not end; God still appoints teachers. Only the apostles and prophets ended with the apostolic era. This was because they were the foundation of the Church (Eph. 2:20; 3:5). The continuing ministries belong to teachers, preachers, teaching-pastors, and evangelists. Teachers were recognized and appointed in the early Church, and given specific positions to teach, even as now. Some of the great professors in evangelical seminaries, some of the great Bible teachers who travel the world—are recognized as divinely appointed teachers, given to the Church.

But any believer may have the gift of teaching and not be appointed to a teaching office in terms of a special ministry to the Church. Many members of the Body have not been called to a ranking position as teachers, but they have the gift of teaching. Basically, teaching is the ability to impart the truths of the Word of God. It's not the same as preaching. Proclaiming the Gospel is one gift; but it is something else to sit down with a newborn babe and instruct him in the things of God. That is the gift of teaching. It can be exercised in a Sunday School class, in a home, or in a counseling situation. Of course, it's possible for a person to have a gift that includes both preaching and teaching.

While teaching is a special gift, every Christian is to some degree a teacher. Every believer is responsible to teach fellow believers, his own family, or others who need the truth (Gal. 6:6; 2 Tim. 2:2, 15).

In the Body, preaching and teaching provide a balanced ministry of evangelism and edification. Preaching is motivating; teaching is instructing. They go side-by-side.

The gift of faith. Faith is one of the Spirit-given gifts. All believers have faith, but some have a special gift of faith. I believe this could just as well be called "the gift of prayer." Faith moves the hand of God.

The gift of wisdom. This is the ability to see deeply into the mysteries of God. It is the kind of insight that sees what the natural eye can't see; that hears what the natural ear cannot hear. It's the ability to take a phrase of Scripture, or a truth of God, pull out of it all the truth, and apply it to life. A simple definition of wisdom is "the application of spiritual truth." Dig it out and put it into practice. In a sense, all believers are to have wisdom (Col. 1:9; James 1:5), but some rise above to minister to the Body in a unique way.

The gift of knowledge. If wisdom is the application of truth, knowledge is understanding the facts. These are the scholars who dig into the Scripture. They research. Some spend all their lives studying ancient manuscripts, archeology, and all kinds of scholarly problems. They are able, by the Spirit of God, to search out the facts. On their work we build our faith. Our Bible didn't drop out of heaven; it took years and years of labor to determine which manuscripts were best.

Knowledge is the academic side of truth; wisdom is application. Some Christians minister both. Some have neither, and some have one. None of these gifts operates according to human ability. Because a man has an IQ of 165 doesn't mean he has the gift of knowledge or the gift of wisdom. Some of the wisest people I have met didn't have an IQ like that. But they had the Spirit-given gift of wisdom. These are spiritual gifts, not intellectual; they are given by a sovereign act of the Holy Spirit. A believer's insights into Scripture do not depend on his IQ.

All Christians are responsible to study to show themselves approved unto God. Both wisdom and knowledge are to belong to every believer (1 Cor. 1:5, 30). And yet, even though we're all to have these spiritual qualities, there is a sense in which some Christians are specially gifted and uniquely called to minister to the Body.

The discernment of spirits. God wanted to protect the Church from false doctrine so He gave certain members of the Body the ability to determine who was right and who was wrong. Some believers have the ability to discern whether spirits are of God or of Satan. The Body faces continual opposition from a host of demons who pose as messengers of light, trying to counterfeit the gifts of the Spirit and sap the energy of the Church. Because of this, God gave certain gifts so that men could discern between God and Satan, something beyond natural insight.

Peter used this gift when he asked Ananias, "Why hath Satan filled thine heart to lie to the Holy Spirit?" (Acts 5:3) How did Peter know? He knew because he had the gift of discernment. Every Christian in a sense is to be discerning. "Beloved, believe not every spirit, but try [test] the spirits whether they are of God: because many false prophets are gone out into the world" (1 John 4:1). Every believer is to be sensitive to spirits, knowing whether they are of God or Satan.

The gift of showing mercy. Next we come to the love gifts. Though all the gifts are to be ministered in love, yet there are three distinct love gifts, that minister to the Body. The first is the gift of showing mercy. Some people can't preach a sermon, but they can do deeds of loving-kindness. This is Christ's love, manifested by the Holy Spirit, through the believers to the Body. It's not just sympathy; it's not exercised out of duty. Some persons have that gift of compassionate love that causes them to do acts of kindness to others. Some of the greatest testimony to Christ is given without a word being spoken; expressing love without saying a thing.

Obviously, all believers are to show deeds of mercy. "If a brother or sister be naked, and destitute of daily food, and one of you say unto them, 'Depart in peace, be ye warmed and filled'; notwithstanding, ye give them not those things which are needful to the body, what does it profit?" (James 2:15–16)

The implication is obvious. All Christians are to be merciful, show kindness, yet some have the gift of showing mercy to the whole body. They set the example for the rest.

The gift of exhortation. The Greek word translated "exhortation" refers to one who comes along to help. Exhortation is not standing in the pulpit browbeating people. It is not necessarily a public gift though it may be used as such (1 Cor. 14:3). It is the ability to get alongside someone and comfort him with love. Jesus said, "I will pray the Father, and He shall give you another Comforter, that He may abide with you forever" (John 14:16).

The Comforter is the Holy Spirit. The word *paracletos* ("Comforter") means "one called alongside." The believer with the gift of exhortation, in the power of the true Paraclete, the Holy Spirit, is used to come alongside members of the Body to comfort, console, encourage, counsel, and exhort. This is the gift that qualifies people to exercise a specially effective personal ministry in the Body. Again, though there are some who have this gift, all Christians are to put their arms around each other every day and comfort, counsel, and share. "But exhort one another daily" (Heb. 3:13).

The gift of giving. This third love gift has direct reference to the material ministry, such as food, clothes, money, or houses. This is a Spirit-given gift, related to the Holy Spirit's supervision of everything a Christian possesses. It doesn't relate at all to how much he has; some with the gift of giving are the poorest. This gift is to provide for others who cannot supply their own needs. If those who have the gift would release themselves and use it in the energy of the Spirit, Christians could take care of all material needs in the Church.

Of course, the Bible commands that no Christian should miss the joy of giving. "Every man according as he purposeth in his heart, so let him give; not grudgingly, or of necessity: for God loveth a cheerful giver" (2 Cor. 9:7).

The gifts of administration. These gifts belong to those in places of spiritual authority. Pastors, teachers, or evangelists exercise this gift. "We beseech you, brethren, to know them which labor among you, and are over you in the Lord, and admonish you" (1 Thes. 5:12).

Some Christians have the place of being over others, to care for them—not to lord it over them, or to hammer them down, or to brutally subject them, but to teach them and instruct them. "Let the elders that rule well be counted worthy of double honor, especially they who labor in the word and doctrine" (1 Tim. 5:17).

The same teaching is found in Hebrews: "Remember them which have the rule over you, who have spoken unto you the Word of God: whose faith follow, considering the end of their conversation [manner of life]. . . . Obey them that have the rule over you, and submit yourselves: for they watch for your souls, as they that must give account. . . . Salute [greet] all them that have the rule over you" (13:7, 17, 24).

The pastor, or elder, who has been given oversight of the flock must exercise the gift of government or ruling. In New Testament terms, I am, in my church, an elder. I'm not a "reverend." I happen to be an elder called by God to teach the Word and, consequently, to have the responsibility of spiritual ruling.

Of course, this gift is not limited to pastors in local churches. It is also exercised by those in leadership in mission societies, youth organizations, and evangelistic associations.

The gift of ministry or helps. Both of these terms mean service; these are gifts of assistance. The early deacons exercised this gift (the word translated "deacon" means service). Christians with this gift are helpers, persons who labor behind the scenes. This gift, like all the others, is to be evident to some degree in all Christians. All Christians are called to serve. "By love serve one another" (Gal. 5:13). Yet some are especially grace-gifted for service to the Body.

We have noted briefly 11 edifying gifts. Every gift was characteristic of Jesus Christ. He was a teacher; He was faithful; He was wisdom personified; He was knowledge; He was the discerner of spirits. He showed mercy; He was the true *paraclete;* He was the giver; He was ruler and leader; and He was servant and minister.

The Church, a new Body formed by Christ, is to do what Christ's fleshly body did—manifest His nature. Since all these gifts were part of His fleshly body, all are also a part of His spiritual Body. These gifts are the reproduction of Christ's ministry. They are now in the new Body of Christ. They are grace gifts (*charismata*) given to the Church by the Holy Spirit, so that the Church may be the continuing life of Christ.

The reason every Christian should share in all these ministries to some degree is that all are called to be like Jesus Christ. Everything that characterized Him should be true also, though imperfectly, of every believer. If the Christian's testimony is to be totally effective, the world will have to see in him the reflection of Jesus Christ Himself. It is vitally important for every believer to know his spiritual gift, and to use it, so that the Body's witness might be effective, and each member in a personal way might show all of Christ's attributes. The key is to allow the Holy Spirit to be in control as we use our gifts.

Temporary Gifts

The temporary gifts were not designed for edifying the Body, but for confirming the testimony of the apostles and prophets, that they were declaring the Word of God. *Four* such gifts are listed in Scripture: miracles, healing, tongues, and interpretation of tongues. They have no continuing role in the Body. They existed for the apostolic era so unbelievers might be convinced that the Word of God was being spoken by the apostles and prophets of the early Church. Certain miraculous gifts were given that people might be convinced that what they heard was true.

And these signs shall follow them that believe; in My
name shall they cast out devils; they shall speak with
new tongues." . . . So then after the Lord had spoken unto them [the apostles], He was received up
into heaven, and sat on the right hand of God. And
they went forth, and preached everywhere, the Lord
working with them, and confirming the Word with
signs following (Mark 16:17, 19-20).

"Signs" *(semeion)* always means "miracles." "Truly the
signs of an apostle were wrought among you in all patience, in
signs, and wonders, and mighty deeds" (2 Cor. 12:12).

The message of salvation initially was spoken by Christ
Himself, and confirmed by the apostles. "God also bearing
them witness" (Heb. 2:4); "them" refers to the apostles. "Both
with signs and wonders, and with divers miracles, and gifts of
the Holy Spirit" (2:4). Apostles did miracles to confirm the
Word. The miracles actually belonged to apostles; certain
gifts of the Spirit were for the apostles. So the miraculous gifts
mentioned (1 Cor. 12:28) are the signs and wonders and
mighty deeds that belonged to the apostles, for the purpose of
establishing the veracity of the Word in the minds of persons
who had no other standard. There was no written Word of
God. There was not yet the accumulated standard of the New
Testament.

In the early Church, the signs were a necessary adjunct to
the preaching and teaching of the apostles and the early
prophets. These gifts were evidently often passed on by the
laying on of hands. In fact, there is no indication in the New
Testament that anyone had these gifts other than by the laying
on of hands of the apostles. B. B. Warfield says,

These miraculous gifts were part of the credentials
of the apostles, as the authoritative agents of God in
founding the church. Their function thus confines
them to distinctly the apostolic Church and they
necessarily passed away with it. Certain passages
specifically associate these miraculous gifts of the
Spirit with the work of apostles. Note this example:

"Long time therefore abode they speaking boldly in the Lord, which gave testimony unto the word of His grace [these were New Testament prophets speaking the Word of the Lord], and granted signs and wonders to be done by their hands" (Acts 14:3).

These words describe the activity of Paul and Barnabas when they went to Iconium during Paul's first missionary journey. God verified His truth by enabling them to do miracles. Note also Romans 15:15-19:

Nevertheless, brethren, I have written the more boldly unto you in some sort, as putting you in mind, because of the grace that is given to me of God, that I should be the minister of Jesus Christ to the Gentiles, ministering the Gospel of God, that the offering up of the Gentiles might be acceptable, being sanctified by the Holy Ghost. I have therefore whereof I may glory through Jesus Christ in those things which pertain to God. For I will not dare to speak of any of those things which Christ hath not wrought by me, to make the Gentiles obedient, by word and deed, through mighty signs and wonders, by the power of the Spirit of God.

From these passages we learn that the purpose and function of the special miraculous gifts of the Spirit was to authenticate the apostles as true messengers from the true God, and thus confirm the Gospel of salvation in the minds of unbelievers. The Church today no longer needs this kind of confirmation. Believers do not need miracles as a standard by which to verify a person's teaching. They don't need someone to stand up and preach, then do a miracle so they will know he's telling the truth. Christians today have the Word of God. When someone preaches, we measure him by the Word of God. If he does not stand that test, we know that he is a false teacher. Abraham told the rich man in hades, "If they hear not Moses and the prophets, neither will they be persuaded, though one rose from the dead" (Luke 16:31). If the Word of God is not sufficient, miracles won't change a person's mind.

Where the written Word of God is available, confirming miracles are irrelevant.

No Emphasis on Miracles

No miraculous confirming gift is mentioned in Ephesians 4, where the gifted men are mentioned. Paul's first letter to the Corinthians is the only one that mentions miraculous temporary gifts. In no letter does he say that pastors, evangelists, or teachers should have any of these gifts. If the confirming gifts of the Word were still needed, they would be given to the men who preach the Word. What would be the point of giving confirming gifts to people who aren't preachers? If, in fact, these gifts still exist, they should belong to the great preachers and teachers in the world, because these are the ones whose message has to be comfirmed. If these gifts were still operative, would they be given to people who are out of the mainstream of the Body, majoring in emotional experiences?

We have seen that the *temporary gift* of signs was for the apostolic era and was never designed to edify the Body.

The gift of miracles. To say that miracles have ceased would be untrue. To say that the gift of miracles has ceased, does not mean that God has stopped performing miracles. God is a God of miracles; He does great miracles today. The greatest kind of miracle God ever does is to take a degenerate soul headed for hell, turn him around, and re-create him so that he becomes a citizen of heaven. But this is not to say that the gift of miracles still exists as a gift through a person. God still does miracles by His own sovereign design and as a result of prayer; but this is not the same as the apostolic gift of miracles.

Jesus did many different kinds of miracles, including raising the dead. They were proofs of His deity. They were to verify His messiahship; they were to substantiate His claim that He is the Son of God. But in His ministry miracles had a very limited effect. Not only did people refuse to believe Him, they also finally concluded that He did His miracles by Beelzebub, Satan.

Miracles also had a limited effect with the apostles and the prophets. In the first place, none of them ever performed a miracle related to natural elements, such as multiplying food or ascending into heaven. The word "miracles" is *duvamis* in Greek, and translates "power." It was the gift of power and can be restricted to the ability to cast out demons (see Matt. 10:1). They were given the ability to cast out demons and to heal. But even this was for a limited time. Paul's restoring of the lame person at Lystra seemed at first to have a great effect on the people, but soon afterward they stoned Paul and left him for dead. Paul's casting out of the evil spirit at Philippi was the direct cause of serious trouble. After this event, for a period of two years, there is no mention of Paul working miracles. There is no record of miracles happening at Antioch, Corinth, Thessalonica, Derbe, or Berea. Paul put no emphasis on them. Instead, he constantly stressed the need for faith. In his list of requirements for bishops, elders, and deacons, he does not mention the gift of miracles. Throughout the epistles there is no emphasis on miracles.

Miracles had no continuing place in the ministry of the Church. They may still occur as God wills, but not through the apostolic *gift* of miracles. The gift of miracles not only had a limited effect, it had a limited purpose. It too was for the infancy stage of the Church, to verify the Gospel. This principle is evident in Scripture. There were four periods of miracles performed by individuals in the Bible: first, in Moses' day; second, in the time of Elijah and Elisha; third, during the life of Christ; and fourth, in the early Church after Pentecost. God performs miracles today, but not to authenticate His Word, and He does them apart from any gift of man. He does them in response to faith and prayer, and according to His own sovereign design.

The gift of healing. The gift of healing was the ability to heal disease and infirmity whenever the opportunity presented itself. Peter said to the lame man, "In the name of Jesus Christ of Nazareth rise up and walk" (Acts 3:6). Peter was able to call on the power of Christ at any time to heal. Healing verified the

Word; it was a confirming gift for unbelievers. God in His grace still heals. We have prayed for people, and God has healed them of diseases when they were beyond recovery medically speaking. However, the gift of healing as such ceased with the apostolic era. Today God heals in His sovereign will in response to the prayer of faith. I believe there is a gift that brings about healing and it is the gift of faith. It is the same as the gift of prayer. God often heals in answer to prayer.

And again, if the gift of healing existed today, it would belong to people who are teachers of the Word. Instead, some who claim the gift of healing are inadequate preachers of the Bible, confused in their theology. They frequently are self-styled "salesmen" operating on a performance basis.

Though we can't deny claims to gifts of healing, it is possible that a person who thinks he has the gift of healing really has the gift of faith and God responds to prayer. My purpose is not to explain all the cases of supposed healing, but rather to indicate the biblical teaching. The true gift of healing was to confirm the teaching and preaching of apostles and prophets.

In the later years of the apostles' ministry the gift of healing began to disappear. The people who were sick stayed sick. God did not heal Paul. Timothy was sick, probably with an ulcer. Did Paul tell him to find one who had the gift of healing? No! He told him to take a little wine. There was the case of Trophimus, who was sick at Miletus (2 Tim. 4:20). Paul left him there, sick. If Paul had the gift of healing (and he had healed previously), would he not have exercised it on behalf of Trophimus?

The Epistle of James was written long before 1 Corinthians, and James tells what to do when somebody gets sick. He does not say, "Go to the healer; find the person who has the gift of healing." Rather, James says, "Is any among you afflicted? Let him pray" (James 5:13). It says *pray*, not call on the man who has the gift of healing. "Let him call for the elders of the church; and let them pray over him, anointing him with oil in the name of the Lord: and the prayer of faith shall save the sick" (5:14-15).

This is thought by many to refer to medicine. James knew by inspiration of the Holy Spirit that in years to come the apostolic gift of healing would not exist. The wisest counsel he could give the Church was to seek by faith the healing that God offers. Having the elders pray and anoint with oil is the biblical approach to healing, especially when the sickness is a result of God's chastening (v. 16).

The gift of healing, like the other temporary gifts, was a sign to unbelievers, and there is no indication in the New Testament Church that the gift of healing was ever experienced by established Christians.

God does heal today, but not by a gift or covenant. It is by His sovereign will in each case. That does not make healing today any less miraculous!

The gift of tongues and the interpretation of tongues. We will cover the third and fourth gifts together (1 Cor. 12:10) and consider several questions related to these gifts.

The gift of tongues was a Holy Spirit-given ability to speak a foreign language to declare the wonderful works of God. It was a miracle of verification.

> And when the day of Pentecost was fully come, they were all with one accord in one place. And suddenly there came a sound from heaven as of a rushing mighty wind, and it filled all the house where they were sitting. And there appeared unto them cloven tongues like as of fire, and it sat upon each of them. And they were all filled with the Holy Ghost, and began to speak with other tongues [the Greek word is *glossa*—languages], as the Spirit gave them utterances (Acts 2:1-4).

Incidents of Tongues-Speaking

It was the Feast of Pentecost. Devout Jews had come to Jerusalem from all over the Roman world. It was seemingly the perfect time to declare the wonderful works of God—at the birth of the Church. Visitors from all over could hear the truth, and take it back to their own countries. So the Christians spoke in all the languages represented. "Now when this was noised abroad, the multitude came together, and were confounded, because every man heard them speak in his own language" (Acts 2:6).

God provided a miracle by which the believers could communicate to persons in their own languages. The miraculous element attested to the truthfulness of the message of Christ's death and resurrection. The people were singularly impressed. " 'We do hear them speak in our tongues [languages] the wonderful works of God.' And they were all amazed and were perplexed, saying one to another, 'What meaneth this?' " (Acts 2:11-12) This means the wonderful works of God were declared.

Speaking in languages did not substitute for preaching, because right after this phenomenon came Peter's sermon. This supernatural event was not necessary to preach the Gospel, and was not used to convict of sin. It attested that God was about to speak. It also was a sign of condemnation on Israel, as Paul shows (1 Cor. 14:21-22).

Elsewhere in Acts, speaking in languages followed the same pattern. It occurred next in Samaria. Previously, the Jews hated the Samaritans, who were a mixed race, but after the Samaritans received the Gospel, the apostles from Jerusalem went to Samaria. When the apostles arrived, they "prayed for them, that they might receive the Holy Ghost: (For as yet He was fallen upon none of them: only they were baptized in the name of the Lord Jesus). Then laid they their hands on them, and they received the Holy Ghost" (Acts 8:15-17).

At that point, I assume, the people spoke in languages otherwise it would have been very easy for the Jewish believers not to accept the Samaritans into fellowship. Tongues demonstrated to the Jewish believers that they might know that the Church was one.

After Samaria, the Gospel reached the Gentile world

through Cornelius. "While Peter yet spake these words, the Holy Ghost fell on all them which heard the Word. And they of the circumcision which believed were astonished" (Acts 10:44-45). The Jews were astonished "because that on the Gentiles also was poured out the gift of the Holy Ghost. For they heard them speak with tongues" (Acts 10:45-46). The Gentiles had the same tongues experience as the Jews at Pentecost. It was important for the Gentiles to have it so that the Jews might know that in the new Body, the Church, everyone was equal. The Holy Spirit and speaking in tongues came on each group whether Jews, Samaritans, or Gentiles.

Acts 19 tells of a handful of people who had been saved under the old economy. They had repented, were baptized by John the Baptist, but did not know about Jesus.

He [Paul] said unto them, "Have ye received the Holy Ghost since ye believed?" And they said unto him, "We have not so much as heard whether there be any Holy Ghost." And he said unto them, "Unto what then were ye baptized?" And they said, "Unto John's baptism." Then said Paul, "John verily baptized with the baptism of repentance, saying unto the people, that they should believe on Him who should come after him, that is, on Christ Jesus." When they heard this, they were baptized in the name of the Lord Jesus. And when Paul had laid his hands upon them, the Holy Ghost came on them; and they spake with tongues (Acts 19:2-6).

Why did these men speak with languages too? Because they needed the same miracle so that all would perceive the unity of the Church. There would be no inequality in the Body. The miracle of tongues occurred those four times in Acts.

The speaking in tongues was always in a known language. It was never gibberish. It was a foreign language known to some present, though the speaker did not know it. The word used in Acts 2 means "language." We read that the Gentiles spoke with tongues and glorified God (Acts 10:46). The witnesses knew the Gentiles were glorifying God because it was a language they understood. Reporting this experience, Peter says, "Forasmuch then as God gave them the like gift as He did unto us" (Acts 11:17). Since the gift was in known languages when the Jews received it, it was in known languages when the Gentiles received it. The same would be true for the disciples of John (Acts 19:6).

Paul speaks of various "kinds of tongues" (1 Cor. 12:10). The word "kinds" is from the word *genos* from which we get our word "genus." *Genos* means a nation, a race, or a kind. "Kinds of tongues" therefore means specific national languages. If tongues is gibberish, Paul's statement would be pointless. How can there be "kinds of gibberish"? Gibberish is gibberish.

Along with speaking in languages is the companion gift of interpreting them. The Greek word literally means "translation," another reason languages can not be merely gibberish. If someone had the gift of speaking known languages, someone else had the gift of translating them. Where the word *unknown* precedes *tongues,* it is always in italics (1 Cor. 14, KJV). This means *unknown* was supplied by the translators, but is not in the original Greek text. Also we read that any use of languages must be according to grammatical structure.

> And even things without life giving sound, whether pipe or harp, except they give a distinction in the sounds, how shall it be known what is piped or harped? (1 Cor. 14:7)

Some Corinthian believers were speaking gibberish; they were exercising a fleshly counterfeit of the real gift. It was a holdover from paganism. Paul used music to prove that speaking in tongues means using a language with grammatical structure.

> Therefore if I know not the meaning of the voice, I shall be unto him that speaketh a barbarian, and he that speaketh shall be a barbarian unto me (14:11).

The miracle of languages was a sign to Jews only. Paul quotes the Prophet Isaiah predicting the gift of tongues as a

God-given sign of condemnation to the Jewish nation. "In the law it is written, 'With men of other tongues and other lips will I speak unto this people; and yet for all that will they not hear Me,' saith the Lord" (14:21).

The expression "this people" can refer only to Israel. When our Lord first came, Israel refused His clear offer of the kingdom. As a result, He spoke to them in parables which they could not interpret (Matt. 13:10-17). As their rejection becomes stronger, after denying the Resurrection, He goes one step further and speaks in a language they can't understand. There was no point for the gift of tongues in the assembly of the Gentile church. Visiting Gentiles would think they were mad (1 Cor. 14:23).

Gifts Abused

It is wrong for Christians today to take the church at Corinth as their pattern for any gift. The Corinthians had perverted the true gifts. The problems in Corinth were many: division, carnality, wrong concepts of the Gospel ministry, sexual perversion, lawsuits between Christians, moral misconduct of believers' bodies, abused marriage relationships, violation of Christian liberty, insubordination of women, evils at the Lord's Supper, ignorance of spiritual gifts, denial of the resurrection of the body.

The Corinthians did not lack spiritual gifts. "Ye come behind in no gift" (1 Cor. 1:7). Rather they abused the gifts. They had a unique problem because in that part of the world ecstatic speech prevailed among the frenzied priests and priestesses of pagan Greek religions. The Corinthian believers had been saved out of that, but evidently they took some of this ecstatic speech into their Christian experience. It was a counterfeit of the true miracle of languages. Paul wrote in an effort to correct the Corinthian abuses which included subordinating preaching.

> Tongues [languages] are for a sign, not to them that believe, but to them that believe not: but prophesying serveth not for them that believe not, but for

them which believe. If therefore the whole church be come together into one place, and all speak with tongues, and there come in those that are unlearned, or unbelievers, will they not say that ye are mad? But if all prophesy, and there come in one that believeth not, or one unlearned, he is convicted of all, he is judged of all (1 Cor. 14:22-24).

The priority of preaching over languages in the church is clearly seen here. Paul goes on to rebuke the believers at Corinth for confusion in their meetings. "If any man speak in an unknown tongue [language], let it be by two, or at the most by three . . . and let one interpret" (14:27). Women were not to speak (14:34).

The big question is whether the miracle of tongues exists today. We should carefully study 1 Corinthians 13:8-12 in this connection.

Charity never faileth: but whether there be prophecies, they shall fail; whether there be tongues [languages], they shall cease; whether there be knowledge, it shall vanish away. For we know in part, and we prophesy in part. But when that which is perfect is come, then that which is in part shall be done away (13:8-10).

Verse 8 indicated that prophecy and knowledge will be "rendered inoperative" *(katargeo)* and tongues will "cease" *(pauo). Pauo* is in the middle voice, which is reflexive—languages will cease "by themselves." The verb is intransitive and doesn't take an object. This means the end of languages is not a great event caused by something else. He meant they would fade by themselves. On the other hand, *katargeo* is a transitive verb; meaning something will cause prophecy and knowledge to cease. That which is "perfect" refers to the return of the Lord.

To illustrate this distinction in a literary way, Paul omits languages from 1 Corinthians 13:9-12 and speaks only of prophecy and knowledge. These gifts will remain unto the glorious consummation; languages will have already ceased.

The evidence of history, according to such scholars as

Warfield, Hoekema, Cotten, and Gromacki, is that the temporary sign gift of languages has ceased.

Why, then, are so many people experiencing the so-called
gift of tongues today? There are several reasons. One is a
departure from systematic Bible interpretation. Many people
don't know any better. Someone convinces them that
"tongues" is the thing to seek. Second, many people are
starved for the supernatural. Tongues gives them a kind of
supernatural experience, something above their usual Christian experience. This leads to the third reason. People want a
feeling of some kind; they want an emotional experience. The
fourth reason people seek this is that they consider it a quick
way to spirituality. Speak in "tongues" and you are spiritual.
They rest in their experience; they go no further.

The modern tongues movement has no basis in biblical
doctrine. Subjective experience is its major defense: "It
happened to me, therefore it must be real." That is not a valid
test. The flesh and Satan can produce counterfeit experiences.

The modern movement confuses the doctrine of the
baptism of the Holy Spirit. A true movement cannot be based
on a false doctrine. "Tongues" people equate speaking
ecstatically with the baptism of the Holy Spirit, but we read,
"For by one Spirit are we all baptized into one body"
(1 Cor. 12:13). That happens at salvation; it is not a continuous thing. Biblically speaking, you can't say to a believer,
"You don't have the Holy Spirit until you speak in tongues."
Every believer has the Spirit. "If any man have not the Spirit of
Christ, he is none of His" (Rom. 8:9). "Know ye not that ye are
the temple of God, and that the Spirit of God dwelleth in you?"
(1 Cor. 3:16)

The new tongues movement also subordinates Christ to the
Holy Spirit. It violates the Spirit's ministry, which is to exalt
Christ. The tongues movement reverses this by making
Christians feel they are "second-class" Christians until they
speak ecstatically. This creates two levels of Christians, the
spiritual ones and the ones who haven't arrived. But in Christ
there is no difference; Christians are one in the Spirit.

All gifts were to be exercised in love. Often, when "tongues" appear in a local church, instead of creating an atmosphere of love, the "gift" creates an atmosphere of friction and division. Any legitimate gift of the Spirit, operated in the energy of the Spirit, brings unity.

Tongues advocates imply that the Church had no power for 1800 years because the Holy Spirit's baptism wasn't experienced. However, we read that believers have "all things that pertain unto life and godliness" (2 Peter 1:3). Believers are not lacking by not having the temporary sign gifts. God made provision for the confirmation of His Word in the nurturing of the infant Church. Today, instead of seeking those things, believers ought to thank God that we don't need them anymore. We have the resources according to the standard of the Word of God. God authenticates His message today by His Word. If God chose to give some miraculous ability today for a special purpose, it must square with all the biblical patterns, for "Jesus Christ [is] the same yesterday, and today, and forever" (Heb. 13:8). Members of the body are not told in Scripture to seek miraculous, temporary, showy "sign" gifts, but rather to minister their permanent gift to edify one another that the Body may grow to full stature.

9
THE FELLOWSHIP
OF THE BODY

(1 John 1:3-10; Acts 2:44-47)

As a human body has connected tissues, muscles, bones, ligaments, and organs, the Body of Christ is comprised of members who are responsible to one another. No member exists detached from the rest of the Body, any more than lungs can lie on the floor in the next room and keep a person breathing. The health of the Body, its witness, and its testimony are dependent on all members faithfully ministering to one another.

As believers in Christ, we are one in position. We have all been placed into the Body of Christ by the Holy Spirit. Positional unity is manifest by the fact that the same Spirit who placed believers into the Body dwells within all believers (1 Cor. 12:13). This is positional unity.

On the other side, we want to discuss practical unity. Though Christians are one in position, unfortunately they are not one in practice—in the nitty-gritty of living and loving together. Positional oneness does not guarantee oneness in practice. Jesus prayed "that they all may be one" (John 17:21). He was praying for Christians to live in oneness.

This practical, experiential unity of the Body is manifest by service and fellowship. By service we mean ministering our spiritual gifts to each other. We have already considered service (chapter 8). Now we turn to the fellowship of sharing our love with each other.

The New Testament word for fellowship is *koinonia*. It means communion or intimate communication. God designed men for fellowship. "It is not good that the man should be alone" (Gen. 2:18). The Church, the Body of Christ, should be the epitome of fellowship. The Church was never intended to be only a building—a place where lonely people walk in, listen, and walk out still alone—but a place of fellowship. In his book *Dare to Live Now!* Bruce Larson says,

> The neighborhood bar is possibly the best counterfeit there is to the fellowship Christ wants to give His Church. It's an imitation, dispensing liquor instead of grace, escape rather than reality. But it is a permissive, accepting, and inclusive fellowship. It is unshockable, it is democratic. You can tell people secrets and they usually don't tell others, or want to. The bar flourishes not because most people are alcoholics, but because God has put into the human heart the desire to know and be known, to love, and be loved, and so many seek a counterfeit at the price of a few beers (Zondervan, p. 110).

This need for fellowship is the genius of the Church. But it is not met simply by attending the Sunday services—whether they be small groups where everyone is known or large congregations where they are not. A desperate need for personal, intimate fellowship exists in the Church today. And this fellowship, like the ministering of the gifts, is intrinsic to manifesting practical unity. Fellowship is essential to the life of the Body. It is body life!

The New Testament teaches four things about fellowship: (1) its basis, (2) its nature, (3) what endangers it, and (4) its responsibilities.

The Basis of Fellowship

There is much phony fellowship today, people getting together on all kinds of pretenses. This is not true Christian fellowship. The basis of body fellowship is not the need of the community, or some common social or religious goal. The basis is found in the word *koinonia,* which suggests sharing and communion—a common ground. Do believers have a common ground? Are they partners in something? Do they have something to share?

We read in 1 John that the ground of Christian fellowship is "that which we have seen and heard declare we unto you, that ye also may have fellowship with us: and truly our fellowship is with the Father, and with His Son Jesus Christ" (1:3).

John relates the Gospel to that which he has personally experienced (1:1). He tells his relationship with Jesus Christ. He proclaims the Gospel because the Gospel is the basis of Christian fellowship. John is saying, "I want you to know the same God and the same Christ I know, in order that we may have common ground for fellowship."

Proclaiming the Gospel is not an end in itself. The preaching of the Gospel creates a fellowship of believers (Phil. 1:5). The beautiful, meaningful fellowship created by Christ and His disciples in the days when He was on earth was not to be limited to them, but was to extend to all of us who came after and believed in Christ. In a sense, we are in the fellowship of the apostles (Ephesians 3 and Hebrews 2) but primarily our fellowship is with the Father and with His Son. We are wrapped up in a total fellowship, involving the Father, the Son, the Spirit, and every other believer in history (Phil. 2:1; 2 Cor. 13:14; Eph. 4:4–6). Salvation made it happen.

There is no fellowship with God prior to salvation, or with Christ or His Spirit. There is no fellowship with believers until we become believers. At that instant we enter fellowship with God and other believers, and it is eternal.

It was God's design to bring us into fellowship. "God is faithful, by whom ye were called unto the fellowship of His Son Jesus Christ our Lord" (1 Cor. 1:9). God is not some distant, cosmic deity. Through His sovereign grace He brought us into His fellowship, by faith in Jesus Christ. Paul speaks of "the common faith" (Titus 1:4). Every believer is part of a common faith, a single body of truth. Each came to God the same way—by faith.

Fellowship in this context becomes a specifically Christian word, referring to a common participation in the eternal life of God by the grace of God, the salvation of Christ, and the blessing of the indwelling Spirit. The objective in all preaching is to create a human fellowship, rising spontaneously out of the divine fellowship. The divine fellowship existed, and because the divine fellowship reached down to man, a human fellowship came into being.

In the purest sense, no Christian is at any time out of fellowship with God, since the relationship is never severed. Suppose, for example, that two enter into marriage. They may not be speaking to each other, yet the partnership continues. Or, partners in business may not like each other, but they remain partners. This is an inadequate way of saying that the believer and God are in an eternal partnership. One may not really be acting like a partner with God—may be violating some of the partnership standards, but the partnership maintains itself. Salvation ushers us into permanent fellowship with God. Paul refers to the "fellowship in the Gospel" which continued "from the first day [salvation]" until the present (Phil. 1:5).

When everything is going great and we are happy and "tuned in" to the Lord, we often say, "I'm in fellowship." When we are not excited about the Lord, and there is sin in our lives and indifference about our Christian experiences, we say, "I'm out of fellowship." Strictly speaking, that is not true. We are always in fellowship but we may not be experiencing the joy of it.

If you want to evaluate your Christian life rightly, say it this way, "I'm experiencing full joy in my fellowship with the Father." Or, "I'm not experiencing the joy of my fellowship with God." "These things write we unto you, that your joy may be full." That is the issue—the difference in the partnership when there is full joy and when there is not full joy (1 John 1:4). The joy of our fellowship with God is affected by sin. If we are not saved, we are out of fellowship, in the theological sense. "If we confess our sins, He is faithful and just to forgive us our sins, and to cleanse us from all unrighteousness" (1 John 1:9). That kind of confession thus becomes the pattern of life. Believers do not need to keep on asking to be forgiven, but by the very nature of their salvation they open their hearts and admit to God what they are—sinful. The unbeliever confesses initially to be saved. A Christian constantly acknowledges his sin. Once he is in fellowship with God, it is the pattern of his life to acknowledge sin, ask forgiveness, and be forgiven.

The Nature of Fellowship

The nature of fellowship may be seen in several New Testament examples.

> And the multitude of them that believed were of one heart and of one soul: neither said any of them that aught [any] of the things which he possessed was his own; but they had all things common. . . . Neither was there any among them that lacked: for as many as were possessors of lands or houses sold them, and brought the prices of the things that were sold, and laid them down at the apostles' feet: and distribution was made unto every man according as he had need (Acts 4:32, 34-35).

These believers shared everything. They had everything in common. That was true fellowship. That fellowship had a marked effect on the world, and as a result, many persons were brought to Christ.

> And all that believed were together, and had all things common; and sold their possessions and goods, and parted them to all men, as every man had need. And they, continuing daily with one accord in the temple, and breaking bread from house to house, did eat their meat with gladness and singleness of heart, praising God, and having favor with all the people. And the Lord added to

the Church daily such as should be saved (Acts 2:44-47).

This was the oneness that Christ had prayed for. Because the world could see this unity and love, people were the more readily convinced of Jesus' identity.

Paul describes a later example of fellowship among churches. "For it hath pleased them of Macedonia and Achaia to make a certain contribution for the poor saints which are at Jerusalem." The wealthier church in Europe collected money to send to poorer Christians. In Christian fellowship there is a spirit of bearing one another's burdens, sharing needs, and teaching (Rom. 1:11-12; Gal. 6:2, 6). Those early Christians enjoyed a fellowship of money, food, homes, prayer, love, spiritual blessing, and teaching.

Paul himself needed this kind of fellowship. He didn't just zip through the world all by himself. "Nevertheless God, that comforteth those that are cast down, comforted us by the coming of Titus" (2 Cor. 7:6). Paul's heart was blessed by fellowship. He told Timothy, "Do thy diligence to come before winter" (2 Tim. 4:21). He cherished fellowship, he longed for it.

What is Christian fellowship today? Is it going to "fellowship hall" in the church basement, to a picnic or a Sunday School class party? Is it a meeting? Fellowship happens when Christians get together to discuss the Word of God and share concerns in the energy of the Holy Spirit. Sometimes after I have been with Christians I write it off as a wasted evening. Other times, I have experienced true fellowship and have come away warmed in spirit.

In true fellowship Christians don't judge one another, they don't bite and devour each other, they don't provoke, envy, lie to one another, speak evil, or grumble about one another. Since true fellowship builds up, Christians receive one another, are kind and tenderhearted to one another, they forbear and forgive one another, serve one another, practice hospitality ungrudgingly to one another, admonish, instruct, submit to one another, comfort one another. That is the true fellowship of the body. It is life touching life to bring blessing and spiritual growth.

The Danger to Fellowship

A believer's fellowship with God is never broken because it is an eternal partnership (John 10:28-29), but since God is holy, sin destroys the joy of the fellowship.

If a Christian sins willfully and continually, he has purposely broken trust with God, has willfully spurned His love. Sin doesn't change God's love, nor does it mean the one who sins doesn't love Him. It does mean that when sin comes in, he loses the joy of communion with God. Usually his prayer life goes, his Bible reading goes, he drifts away from other Christians and their relationships—all because he doesn't want to be confronted with God.

The symbol of Body fellowship is the Communion service. When Christians meet around the Lord's table and partake of the cup and the bread, they are symbolizing His death which is the basis of fellowship. The word *koinonia* in Greek includes both fellowship and Communion. Paul writes,

> The cup of blessing which we bless, is it not the communion of the blood of Christ? The bread which we break, is it not the communion of the body of Christ? . . . Ye cannot drink the cup of the Lord, and the cup of devils; ye cannot be partakers of the Lord's table, and of the table of devils (1 Cor. 10:16, 21).

How could Christians drink of the cup of the Lord, celebrate their fellowship with Him, and then go out and fellowship with demons? That makes a mockery of the Cross. Sin is communion with Satan and his fallen angels. It is blasphemous to do that while also going to the Lord's table. So Paul warns, "Let a man examine himself, and so let him eat of that bread, and drink of that cup. For he that eateth and drinketh unworthily, eateth and drinketh damnation to himself, not discerning the Lord's body" (1 Cor. 11:28-29).

How does God judge a believer who does that? "For this

cause many are weak and sickly among you, and many sleep" (11:30). Some of them even died. The Lord's table is the best-known example of Christian fellowship because it symbolizes the Cross which brought believers into the fellowship. When a believer was living in a pattern of sin, he was thereby forbidden to enter into this experience of Communion. Why? Because his sin had violated all that the Cross stood for, his participation would have been a mockery serious enough, in fact, to cause his own death. That is why Paul warns us not to go to the Lord's table without examining ourselves to be sure that we are not at the same time celebrating or fellowshiping with demons.

Sin breaks the joy of a Christian's fellowship with other believers as well as with the Lord. It shatters the unity of the body. Your sin affects me because it limits my fellowship, and it limits the use of your gifts in my behalf. A Christian can't say, "I can do what I want, it won't affect anybody else." Sin in a believer's life causes a crippling of the Body, by eliminating fellowship which is so needed. Pride, lust, materialism, failure to minister one's gift, ceasing to pray, spiritual laziness, not yielding to the Holy Spirit—all these and every other sin destroy fellowship in the Body.

If one acknowledges his sin and confesses it to God, it will not become the pattern and thus not affect the fellowship as continuous, prolonged sin does. I find that if I sin and immediately acknowledge my sin to God and repent, the joy of my fellowship is unbroken. But when sin persists, the joy of fellowship is destroyed. The danger to fellowship, then, is sin without repentance. We see that the basis of fellowship is salvation, the nature of it is unity, and the danger to it is sin.

The Responsibilities of Fellowship
What is our obligation to other believers in terms of fellowship? We maintain fellowship by doing specific deeds for other believers. They are the "one anothers" of the New Testament.

"Confess your faults one to another, and pray one for another" (James 5:16). The word translated "fault" is the

Greek word *hamartia,* the chief New Testament word for sin. One way to maintain the fellowship of the Body of Christ is to confess our sins to other Christians. Imagine what a depth of honesty, beauty, and understanding would be brought to Christian fellowship if believers could openly share their sins. They ought to be able to know that when they share problems their fellow Christians will often say, "That's amazing; I have the same problem." Believers could more intelligently pray for and minister to each other if they knew they had the same problems.

Too often, however, Christians put little glass bubbles around themselves and try to look like super-saints, as if they hadn't a problem in the world. They are not willing to share openly, to expose their sins and problems to a fellow believer. They don't know what it is to have another believer say, "That's the same thing I'm going through. You pray for me and I'll pray for you." Recently a brother in Christ confessed a sin to me and promised to tell me each time he committed it. Later he told me that promise prevented him from committing the sin again.

James knew what he was talking about when he said, "Confess your faults one to another." That may not be only good psychological therapy, but spiritually it is a tremendous preventative to sin. Somewhere along the line Christians need to break through their isolation, crucify their egos, and begin to share and confess their faults one to another. There is no priesthood here except the priesthood of believers. This confession is *one* believer to *one* other—not publicly before either the whole Church or the world.

If a believer has wronged a fellow believer he should go to him. "Therefore if thou bring thy gift to the altar, and there rememberest that thy brother hath aught [anything] against thee; leave there thy gift before the altar, and go thy way; first be reconciled to thy brother, and then come and offer thy gift" (Matt. 5:23-24). You don't pay homage to God until you have made everything right with other believers.

Confession of sin to each other results in a more pure

fellowship of people who know and love each other and understand each other's needs, anxieties, temptations, and sins. Each Christian has this responsibility in the Body. What strength Christians would find in such a community!

Forgive One Another

Not only do Christians confess their sins one to another, but they forgive one another. Some Christians have a hard time doing that. You hear them say, "Well, if somebody ever did that to me, I'd never forgive him!" Such an attitude is unworthy of a Christian.

"Sufficient to such a man is this punishment" (2 Cor. 2:6). This means that fellow Christians are not to hold sin over a brother's head the rest of his life. On the contrary, "ye ought rather to forgive him, and comfort him, lest perhaps such a one should be swallowed up with overmuch sorrow. Wherefore I beseech you that ye would confirm your love toward him" (2:7–8).

If a person is taken in sin, he will have enough problems with the consequences of sin without other Christians holding it over his head. They are to go to him and forgive him.

Paul adds, "Forbearing one another, and forgiving one another, if any man have a quarrel against any; even as Christ forgave you" (Col. 3:13). No one deserves to be forgiven by Christ. So it is not right to accept Christ's forgiveness and then refuse to extend forgiveness to a fellow Christian (Eph. 4:32).

Forgiveness balances confession. When someone comes and confesses, you forgive. If someone confesses, "I just want you to know that for 10 years I have hated you. I've been talking behind your back," the Christian reaction should be forgiveness. When there is that kind of mutual concern in the Body of Christ, great things will happen.

Bear One Another's Burdens

"Bear ye one another's burdens, and so fulfill the law of Christ" (Gal. 6:2). A Christian can't bear someone's burden unless that person shares it. Christians start by confessing their faults, forgiving each other, and then carrying each other's burdens. This means sympathetically loving one another.

What should a Christian do when he sees a believer sinning? Don't say anything to him? Don't embarrass him? In Ephesians we read, "And have no fellowship with the unfruitful works of darkness, but rather reprove them" (5:11). If a Christian sees a brother who is sinning he has the spiritual obligation to tell him so—in love (see Matt. 18:15). This is a serious thing. Paul says, even in reference to an elder, "Them that sin rebuke before all, that others also may fear" (1 Tim. 5:20). It may even come to putting them out of the church (Matt. 18:17; 1 Cor. 5:5).

Imagine what would happen if I called Mr. So-and-so in front of others and said, "Now I want to tell you what you did. . . ." If our fellowship in the Body were really working, this would tend to have an immediate purifying effect on us all. However, most Christians are afraid to exercise this responsibility. If they discover someone else's sin, they gasp and keep it to themselves, or they gossip about it.

Occasionally, someone will come to me and say, "You know, Pastor, I don't know if you've heard, but Mr. So-and-so is doing such-and-such." When that happens, I say, "Have you talked to him about it?"

If a Christian sees a brother in a sin, he is to rebuke him, remembering that the brother has the same obligation. The point of this is not only to restrict sin, but also to get Christians to open up and be themselves with each other. The Church is a fellowship where every body-member ministers. We need to be ready to rebuke sin in each other. Paul said to Titus in regard to certain Christians in Crete: "Wherefore rebuke them sharply, that they may be sound in the faith" (Titus 1:13). If we find someone teaching false doctrine we are to tell him so. "These things speak, and exhort, and rebuke with all authority. Let no man despise thee" (Titus 2:15).

The Christian who is Spirit-filled has the right to go to a sinning brother and openly rebuke him for his sins. That leads to pure fellowship. Once we have rebuked him, and he repents truly, it is time to restore him. "If a man be overtaken in a fault, ye which are spiritual, restore such an one in the spirit of meekness; considering thyself, lest thou also be tempted" (Gal. 6:1). Pick him up and say, "Now let me show you from the Word of God what is going on. Let's have prayer together. Let's get back on the right track." That is restoring, caring for him. A Christian hasn't done his duty if he stops with rebuke. He needs to restore, in love.

We are to take special care of the weaker brother—not to offend him. We are not to abuse liberty and cause offense (Rom. 14:13, 19).

Loving equally with no favoritism is the theme of Paul's thought (Rom. 12:10, 16; 13:8; 15:5, 7) and it is the central thrust of Christian fellowship. The fellowship of the Body is shattered when love has preference. We must cultivate love for all, without favorites. This means esteeming all above ourselves. John said, "Beloved, let us love one another" (1 John 4:7).

Peter called for this when he wrote, "See that ye love one another with a pure heart fervently" (1 Peter 1:22). "Fervently" is a word from the medical vocabulary; it means "stretched." Christians are to stretch their love like an extended muscle to reach all. Peter further defined this kind of equal, stretched love as compassionate (3:8), hospitable to strangers (4:9), submissive (5:5), and physically demonstrative (5:14).

This kind of love should include caring service for each other (Gal. 5:13); patience and long-suffering (Eph. 4:2; Col. 3:13); and result in kindness, tenderheartedness, and forgiveness (Eph. 4:32; Col. 3:13).

Comforting and exhorting one another are mentioned in several Scriptures. Paul, writing to the discouraged Thessalonian believers, encouraged them to "comfort one another" (1 Thes. 4:18; 5:11). Twice in Hebrews we read "exhort one another" (3:13; 10:25). "Comfort" and "exhort" come from the same Greek word, *parakaleo*. It means "to come alongside to help." This is the ministry of personal care. It is presented in light of the brevity of time. In Thessalonians, it is in the context of the Rapture; in Hebrews, of coming judgment. It is an urgent word. Christians are to help each other in view of the coming of Jesus (Rev. 22:12).

The responsibility of discipline belongs not only to the individual, but may come to the local assembly. The local church has the responsibility, when someone continues in sin, to put that person out of the church. Paul told the Corinthians "to deliver such an one unto Satan" (1 Cor. 5:5). Paul told Timothy that he was delivering Hymenaeus and Alexander to Satan, that they might learn not to blaspheme (1 Tim. 1:20). We usually think the sinning believer needs to be in church, but the Bible says to put him out. Sin destroys the purity of the fellowship! Jesus gives the pattern for such dismissal. A believer continuing in sin must be brought to the place of repentance before God. The Body cannot tolerate sin. In the early Church, sinning brothers were put out in two ways: they were eliminated from the Lord's table, and they were put out of the fellowship of other believers. They were still regarded as Christians, but they were removed lest they taint the fellowship.

Three "one anothers" make a fitting conclusion for this chapter. The first one is to "edify one another" (Rom. 14:19; 1 Thes. 5:11). The tool for this is the Word of God. Paul commended the Ephesian elders "to God, and to the word of His grace, which is able to build you up" (Acts 20:32). Christians have a far-reaching responsibility to know the Word, not only for their own sakes but so they can build up each other. Personal ignorance of Scripture brings damage to the Body.

The second is "to admonish one another" (Rom. 15:14; Col. 3:16). Apparently, this kind of encouraging counsel implies sin is present. It means encouraging a brother in sin to live righteously and godly. Admonishing is never harsh, unloving, or abusive. It is to be done gently (2 Thes. 3:14-15).

The third "one another" is "pray one for another" (James 5:16). This responsibility is at the heart of relationships in the Body. It is something no Christian may avoid and still be a contributing member of the Body. Such mutual prayer is based on the honest sharing of personal needs and the personal discipline involved in setting a regular time for it.

In summary, fellowship in the Body results in joy. Christ came to give believers full joy (John 16:24)—joy resulting from pure fellowship with God and with one another. Such fellowship is possible; God planned it that way. It is each Christian's responsibility to make fellowship in the Body all that God intends it to be.

10
THE WITNESS
OF THE BODY

(John 15:26-27)

The principle on which the Body operates is humility. The mark which distinguishes the Body is love. The service of the Body is to minister spiritual gifts. The fellowship of the Body is to share love. The purpose for which God created the Body is to be a channel through which He can accomplish His will—the redemption of His people. More exactly defined, then, the Body is to be edified in order that it might witness to the world.

From the beginning God has desired to communicate with man, to manifest His truth to man. His crowning act of communication was sending Jesus Christ into the world. After His death and resurrection, He ascended into heaven and is no longer visible on earth. But God, through Christ, sent the Holy Spirit to manifest Himself in another Body—the Body of Christ, the Church. This time it was not one body physically, but many bodies, making up one spiritual Body. In the Church, Christ continues to dwell, through the Spirit. Christ is in the Body, manifesting His glory and all His attributes, just as He did in His human body when He was here for 33 years. When Christ's physical body was here, He manifested love, holiness, wisdom, power, and all the glory of God. In this new Body, the Church, He wants to manifest the very same attributes. Christians, as the Body of Christ, are to manifest Christ.

God's will for this earthly Body, is that all members "come in the unity of the faith, and of the knowledge of the Son of God . . . unto the measure of the stature of the fullness of Christ" (Eph. 4:13).

We read that God has predestinated believers to be conformed to the image of His Son (Rom. 8:28-29). Grasp the miraculous nature of this statement. Christ can take our human bodies, subject to sin and death, physically frail, and make them into His temple—literally dwelling in them, planting in them His glory, that they might manifest Him to the world. What a miracle! What a demonstration of God's power in love.

Here is the key. Through this Body, this unity of all believers, Christ wants to manifest the mighty victorious power of His person. As a Body, believers are to manifest Christ to the world. They are called together to be mature and edified, taught and built up that they can witness to the world. The Body has diverse gifts for its edification and maturity. The more believers use these diverse gifts, the more obvious unity will become. The more we minister to each other with our gifts, the more we become one, and the more the world can see our oneness. When the world sees Christian oneness, people will know that Christ came from God.

This does not mean an individual member is excused from being a witness. People have said to me, "I don't think the Lord has called me to be a witness." Every member of the Body is to witness. "Ye shall receive power," said Jesus, "after that the Holy Ghost is come upon you: and ye shall be witnesses unto Me." There is no option. "Therefore if any man be in Christ, he is a new creature; old things are passed away; behold, all things are become new. And all things are of God, who hath reconciled us to Himself by Jesus Christ and hath given to us the ministry of reconciliation" (2 Cor. 5:17-18). Anyone reconciled to Christ has the ministry of communicating reconciliation to others. No Christian is excused. In the same chapter we read, "Now then we are ambassadors for Christ, as though God did beseech you by us: we beg you in Christ's stead, be ye reconciled to God" (5:20). Christians need to be sensitive to the truth of the New Testament about the nature of witness—as members and as a total Body.

A key text dealing with this is in John: "But when the Comforter is come, whom I will send unto you from the Father, even the Spirit of Truth, which proceedeth from the Father, He shall testify of Me: And ye also shall bear witness, because ye have been with Me from the beginning" (15:26-27).

On Trial

In those two verses we discover the basic concept of the Body's witness. The word "witness" is interesting, in that it takes us into a law court. We see a judge on the bench and a prisoner on trial. We hear the case argued by the prosecution, then by the defense. Both call witnesses to substantiate their cases. The setting implies that Christians, as individual members of the Body, are witnesses in a trial, so to speak. Jesus Christ is on trial. The judge is the world. The defense attorney is the Holy Spirit. The prosecutor is Satan with his lies and accusations. Christians are witnesses.

Believers are witnesses in a situation where Jesus Christ is on trial before the world—not before the Sanhedrin, not before Pilate, and not before Herod Antipas. Jesus is on trial at the bar of world opinion. The world judges Christ on the basis of the witnesses. Some people judge Him to be a fake; some judge Him to be a good man; others judge Him to be a teacher; others, a liar, and so on. If a witness tears down the claims of Jesus Christ by the kind of life he lives, it would be better if he were out of the courtroom altogether. He only confuses the issue. The word "comforter" is *paracletos,* "one called alongside for defense." The Holy Spirit defends Christ. He calls members of the Body to witness and confirm the testimony of Christ (John 15:27). All Christians are witnesses, either helping or hindering the cause of Christ.

The Body witnesses by its unity (John 13:34-35; 17:7). Can you imagine the impact that a united Church would have on this world? I don't mean an ecumenical church where everybody kisses doctrine good-bye, throws their arms around each other, and marches off to battle over the latest social issue. The Body of Christ comprising true believers needs to be one. Sadly, it is not. Today the Body's testimony in that regard is pathetically weak. Our testimony too often is strife, division, carnality, and confusion. The world, then, renders its verdict on the strength of these two kinds of witnesses: the individual members of the Body, and the Body as a whole.

We will examine in this chapter six aspects of the Body's witness: (1) to the world; (2) of the Son; (3) by the Father; (4) through the Holy Spirit; (5) in the individual member; (6) in the total body.

Witness Is to the World

Christians will not understand the nature of their witnesses until they understand what the world is. Jesus spoke about its characteristics. Generated and controlled by Satan, "the world" is the entire system of evil which operates on the earth through demons and men who don't know God (John 8:44). The prince and ruler of this world is the devil—the whole world is in his power. True, the world is passing away (1 John 2:17) but while it lasts, it is the absolute antagonist of the Church. The world hates the Church, and its hatred is deep and bitter.

The verses about the Body's witness are in a context of the world's hostility and hatred.

> If the world hate you, ye know that it hated Me before it hated you. If ye were of the world, the world would love his own: but because ye are not of the world, but I have chosen you out of the world, therefore the world hateth you. . . . But all these things will they do unto you for My name's sake, because they know not Him that sent Me. . . . If I had not done among them the works which none other man did, they had not had sin: but now have they both seen and hated

both Me and My Father. But this cometh to pass, that the word might be fulfilled that is written in their law, They hated Me without a cause. . . . These things have I spoken unto you, that ye should not be offended. They shall put you out of the synagogues: yea, the time cometh, that whosoever killeth you will think that he doeth God service. And these things will they do unto you, because they have not known the Father, nor Me (John 15:18-19, 21, 24-25; 16:1-3).

The world hates, the world ostracizes, the world kills. The world is antagonistic. But Jesus goes on to say that believers must witness to the world. Note the word, "But"! (15:26) "But when the Comforter is come," you will confront the world and witness to it.

How is a member of the Body to react when he is faced with the opposition of the world? If they throw him out, if he is cursed, what is he to do? Retaliate in anger? No! Lick his wounds in self-pity? No! Withdraw and go back to Bible study? No! He is supposed to bear witness before the world whatever the cost—and count it all joy to suffer in Jesus Christ's place (Col. 1:24).

Witness Is of the Son

"And ye also shall bear witness, because ye have been with Me" (John 15:27). The world's hatred focuses on Jesus Christ. "They hated Me without a cause" (15:25). Christ is on trial, and Christian testimony must be of Him.

Preaching centers on Jesus Christ throughout the New Testament. In Revelation we read, "Who bare record [bore witness] of the Word of God, and of the testimony of Jesus Christ" (1:2). John's testimony was Christ. Later he reiterates the idea: "And the dragon was wroth with the woman, and went to make war with the remnant of her seed, which keep the commandments of God, and have the testimony of Jesus Christ" (12:17). Testimony was always directly associated with Jesus Christ. In fact, we also read that the Old Testament witnessed to Christ: "For the testimony of Jesus is the spirit of prophecy" (19:10).

The apostles had no doubts about this. Jesus told them before and after His death and resurrection that they were to testify of Him. "Ye shall be witnesses unto Me" (Acts 1:8). They obeyed. Their sermons in the early Church were always about Jesus Christ. Peter preached to Cornelius and said, "God anointed Jesus of Nazareth with the Holy Ghost and with power: who went about doing good, and healing all that were oppressed of the devil; for God was with Him. And we are witnesses of all things which He did both in the land of the Jews, and in Jerusalem; whom they slew and hanged on a tree: Him God raised up the third day, and showed Him openly" (Acts 10:38-40). Peter's sermons were always about Jesus.

Much so-called witnessing has nothing to do with Jesus Christ. It talks about religion or about the church, or vaguely about God.

We say, "I witnessed to my friend."

"What did you say?"

"Well, I kind of let him know that I go to church."

Often our witnessing is only an autobiography, and we never get around to Christ. We give our spiritual life history. A Christian can give his entire "testimony" and the listener might know nothing more about Jesus than when the Christian started. Witnessing is through testimony to Jesus Christ! It is proclaiming the great truths of His virgin birth, sinless life, atoning death, physical resurrection, ascension, and coming again.

Witness Is by the Father

"When the Comforter is come, whom I will send to you from the Father" (John 15:26). When Jesus Christ sent the Spirit, He really sent God's witness to this world. For the Spirit proceeded from the Father and bore the Father's testimony. The Father is the Son's chief witness. It was the Father's supreme concern to bring honor and glory to the Son. Jesus answered the Jews' question about His identity by saying, "If I honor myself, My honor is nothing; it is My Father that honoreth Me" (John 8:54). See this also:

> If I bear witness of Myself, My witness is not true. There is another that beareth witness of Me; and I know that the witness which He witnesseth of Me is true. . . . But I have greater witness than that of John: for the works which the Father hath given Me to finish, the same works that I do, bear witness of Me, that the Father hath sent Me. And the Father Himself, which hath sent Me, hath borne witness of Me (John 5:31-32, 36-37).

Jesus said, in effect, "The Father is My chief witness. He is the one primarily concerned with communicating who I am. The Spirit who proceeds from the Father is sent to carry the Father's witness and plant it within you!"

How did the Father bear witness to the Son? First, through the Old Testament. "Search the Scriptures," Jesus said to the Jews, "for in them ye think ye have eternal life: and they are they which testify of Me" (John 5:39). Jesus revealed this to the disciples on the road to Emmaus: "And beginning at Moses and all the prophets, He expounded unto them in all the Scriptures the things concerning Himself" (Luke 24:27).

The second way in which God witnessed to His Son was through Christ's works. "Jesus answered them, I told you, and ye believed not: the works that I do in My Father's name, they bear witness of Me" (John 10:25). The miracles that Jesus did were the Father's witness. They showed that Jesus is who He claimed to be. "Believest thou not that I am in the Father, and the Father in Me? The words that I speak unto you, I speak not of Myself: but the Father that dwelleth in Me, He doeth the works" (John 14:10). The works that Christ did were actually the works of the Father attesting to His claim to deity.

The third means of the Father's witness was by direct speaking. God actually said: "This is My beloved Son" (Matt. 17:5). The Father, then, is the source of all witness about Christ. That entire witness is recorded in Scripture: The

Old Testament prophecies, the works that Jesus did, the words that He spoke, the direct statements of the Father. Christian witness should be an echo of the Father's witness. Believers should study the Word diligently, to really know the Father's witness.

Witness Is through the Spirit

"But when the Comforter is come, whom I will send unto you from the Father, even the Spirit of Truth, which proceedeth from the Father, He shall testify of me" (John 15:26). Whatever witness God the Father has in the world, He has through the Holy Spirit. The Holy Spirit has two names, "Comforter" and "Spirit of Truth." The Holy Spirit calls believers into court to testify. Since He is also "the Spirit of Truth," this reveals the kind of testimony He gives. He cannot be a false witness; He is truth and always declares truth. Jesus ministered in the power of the Spirit, and Christians cannot witness apart from Him.

Where does the Spirit dwell today? In believers. They are the vehicle carrying the witness that proceeds from the Father by the Spirit. The Holy Spirit has no physical voice. His witnessing is through members of the Body. When Jesus promised to send the Holy Spirit, He said, "He dwelleth with you, and shall be in you" (14:17). We read, "They [believers] were all filled with the Holy Ghost, and they spake the Word of God with boldness" (Acts 4:31). Members of the body are individual witnesses, empowered by the resident Holy Spirit. Witnessing, then, is carrying the testimony of the Father brought to us through the Spirit, and communicating it to the world.

Christians are qualified to witness not only because of the resident Holy Spirit, but also because they have experienced Jesus Christ firsthand. Christ's words were directed to the disciples gathered with Him in the Upper Room (John 15), but they also apply to believers today. We can be witnesses only if we experience what we are testifying about. To witness in a court case we must have been personally involved; second-hand testimony is unacceptable.

I will never forget when I had to go to court to testify about a crime I had seen. They asked me three things: "What did you see?" "What did you hear?" "What did you feel?" A witness is someone with firsthand experience—I heard it, I saw it, and I felt it. I was there. "That which . . . we have heard, which we have seen with our eyes . . . and our hands have handled, of the Word of life . . . declare we unto you" (1 John 1:1, 3).

It is a witness to say, "I have been with Jesus Christ. I have seen Him, heard Him, and I have touched Him." Then you are a qualified witness. Body witness is not a detached lecture about Jesus; it is to say, "I have seen and heard the Christ and He has touched my life."

Down through the ages this kind of character witness has been more precious than life itself. The word *martus,* which means "witness," came to mean "martyr," because many times when believers were standing up as witnesses for Christ, it cost them their lives. The Body of Christ needs more who will witness effectively, whatever the cost to their egos or their lives.

Witness Is in the Body
The Holy Spirit indwells not only every individual member, but also the entire, collective Body, the Church.

> For He is our peace, who hath made both one [Jew and Gentile], and hath broken down the middle wall of partition between us; Having abolished in His flesh the enmity [that is, the antagonism between Jew and Gentile], even the law of commandments contained in ordinances; for to make in Himself of twain one new man . . . For through Him we both have access by one Spirit unto the Father. . . . In whom all the building fitly framed together groweth unto an holy temple in the Lord; In whom ye [plural] also are builded together for an habitation of God through the Spirit (Eph. 2:14-15, 18, 21-22).

The entire Church, the Body of Christ, is the temple of the Holy Spirit, just as the individual member is. The Holy Spirit indwells the total Body in order to carry the witness of the Father planted in the Body to the world.

How can the Body witness in a collective, single testimony? There are two ways. First, the Body witnesses by its visible oneness. Jesus prayed, "Neither pray I for these [disciples] alone, but for them also which shall believe on Me through their word; that they all may be one; as Thou Father, art in Me, and I in Thee, that they also may be one in Us; that the world may believe that Thou hast sent Me" (John 17:20-21).

Today this Body witness is not from a unified Body. We are fragmented, each group trying to protect its own ideas. We haven't begun to see what God can do through a united testimony to Jesus in the Church. What an impact we would make if only the world could see us as one.

The second way the Body witnesses is by love. "Little children, yet a little while I am with you. Ye shall seek Me: and as I said unto the Jews, Whither I go, ye cannot come; so now I say to you. A new commandment I give unto you, That ye love one another; as I have loved you, that ye also love one another. By this shall all men know that ye are My disciples, if ye have love one to another" (John 13:33-35). Christians would have a powerful effect on this world if they showed love for one another.

Individual Body members are the last link in the witness of the Father. The testimony started with the Father, about the Son, through the Spirit, and came to us. The testimony of Christ must not break down at this level. Each Christian as a Body member must do his part to witness. Each one must help to create oneness by ministering his spiritual gift, by loving, and by fulfilling the demands of fellowship. Then the mission of the Father in sending the Son will come to pass as God intended. There is a world to be won; it will be won, as we are one!

Epilogue

PERSONALIZING THE PRINCIPLES

The following statement is attributed to Aristides, a second-century worldly philosopher. It is his comment on Christians:

They abstain from all impurity, in the hope of the recompense that is to come in another world. As for their servants or handmaids or children, they persuade them to become Christians by the love they have for them; and when they have become so, they call them without distinction, brothers. They do not worship strange gods; and they walk in all humility and kindness and falsehood is not found among them and they love one another. When they see the stranger they bring him to their homes and rejoice over him as over a true brother; for they do not call brothers those who are after the flesh, but those who are in the Spirit and in God.

And there is among them a man that is poor and needy and if they have not an abundance of necessities, they fast two or three days that they may supply the needy with the necessary food.

They observe scrupulously the commandment of their Messiah; they live honestly and soberly as the Lord their God commanded them. Every morning and all hours on account of the goodness of God toward them, they praise and laud Him and over their food and their drink, they render Him thanks.

And if any righteous person of their number passes away from this world, they rejoice and give thanks to God and they follow his body as though he were moving from one place to another. And when a child is born to them, they praise God, and if again it chances to die in its infancy, they praise God mightily, as for one who has passed through the world without sins.

Such is the law of the Christians and such is their conduct (Aristides, "The Apology of Aristides," *Encyclopedia Britannica,* Vol. 1, p. 346).

This can be so today. It must be! God's blueprint for the Body is clear. But all the plans are useless, unfulfilled, unless you and I make them part of our lives.

Part of a Masterpiece

Commitment involves a personal vow on our part to exercise the priorities God has laid down for the building of Christ's Body. We must be willing to aggressively dedicate ourselves to answer the prayer of our Lord for unity. We must realize we are a strategic part of a great masterpiece.

There is a famous story from the days when Sir Christopher Wren was building St. Paul's cathedral in London. Wren was making a tour one day and asked a man working on the building, "What are you doing?"

The workman replied, "I am cutting this stone to the right size."

He asked a second man working elsewhere, "What are you doing?"

"I am earning money," he retorted.

When Wren asked a third man, the man paused from his work and excitedly replied, "I am helping Sir Christopher Wren to build St. Paul's cathedral!"

As Christians, we must hold before us the loftiest ideal of our presence in the Church—we are here, in the Spirit's energy, working to help the Lord Jesus Christ build His Church. To this we must be committed.

Since the principles are revealed only in the Word of God, diligent and systematic study is essential, not only for initial information and inspiration, but for review, that we may be constantly remembering these priorities.

These truths must be taught from the pulpit, in Sunday School and Bible studies, through personal discipling, and family devotions. The Church for too long has allowed the truths to lie dormant. We must teach.

It is most sobering to realize that the whole plan for the Church depends on us for its accomplishment. It all comes down to whether we are faithful to commitment, careful study, and communication.

> Finally, brethren, farewell. Be perfect, be of good comfort, be of one mind, live in peace; and the God of love and peace shall be with you. Greet one another with an holy kiss. All the saints salute you. The grace of the Lord Jesus Christ, and the love of God, and the communion of the Holy Ghost be with you all. Amen (2 Cor. 13:11–14).